BECOMING CULTURALLY ORIENTED

BECOMING CULTURALLY ORIENTED

Practical Advice for Psychologists and Educators

Nadya A. Fouad and Patricia Arredondo

American Psychological Association
Washington, DC

Published by
American Psychological Association
750 First Street, NE
Washington, DC 20002
www.apa.org

To order
APA Order Department
P.O. Box 92984
Washington, DC 20090-2984
Tel: (800) 374-2721; Direct: (202) 336-5510
Fax: (202) 336-5502; TDD/TTY: (202) 336-6123
Online: www.apa.org/books/
E-mail: order@apa.org

In the U.K., Europe, Africa, and the Middle East, copies may be ordered from
American Psychological Association
3 Henrietta Street
Covent Garden, London
WC2E 8LU England

Typeset in Meridien by Stephen McDougal, Mechanicsville, MD

Printer: United Book Press, Inc., Baltimore, MD
Cover Designer: Aqueous Design, Bethesda, MD
Technical/Production Editor: Kristen S. Boye

The opinions and statements published are the responsibility of the authors, and such opinions and statements do not necessarily represent the policies of the American Psychological Association.

Library of Congress Cataloging-in-Publication Data

Fouad, Nadya A.
  Becoming culturally oriented : practical advice for psychologists and educators / by Nadya A. Fouad and Patricia Arredondo.
     p. cm.
  Includes bibliographical references and index.
  ISBN-13: 978-1-59147-424-1
  ISBN-10: 1-59147-424-8
  1. Cross-cultural counseling. I. Arredondo, Patricia M. II. Title.

  BF637.C6F576 2007
  158'.3—dc22   2006009700

British Library Cataloguing-in-Publication Data
A CIP record is available from the British Library.

Printed in the United States of America
First Edition

Contents

6

Implications for Psychologists as Researchers   81

7

Psychologists as Organizational Change Agents   95

BECOMING
CULTURALLY
ORIENTED

Introduction to Multicultural-Centered Practices

1

Be the change you wish to see in the world.

—Mahatma Gandhi

s a whole, the United States is increasingly becoming more racially and ethnically diverse, which is and will be reflected in a multicultural student body, client population, research participants, and organizational communities. It is critical for psychologists to become culturally oriented, or they run the risk of not providing effective services to clients, poorly educating students, doing harm with their research, or losing the opportunity to serve as advocates. This book is designed to help psychologists learn about the role of culture in the various roles they play—practitioners, educators, researchers, and organizational change agents—and to help them become culturally oriented in their work.

There are a number of reasons for psychologists to become culturally oriented, including the most pragmatic reason: If we do not understand ourselves and others as cultural beings, we will increasingly be out of touch with the reality of the marketplace and not be viewed as providing valuable services. In short, the psychologist who is culturally myopic runs the risk of unemployment. There is also an ethical imperative to be culturally oriented: the American Psychological Association's (APA's) "Ethical Principles of Psychologists and Code of Conduct" (APA, 2002; see also APA Web site version at http://www.apa.org/ethics/) prompts psychologists to be concerned to do no harm (Principle A), to provide equal quality of services to all (Principle D), and to respect others' rights and dignity (Principle E).

We believe, though, that psychologists may be most moved by the general principle of equity and fairness to become culturally oriented.

Guthrie (1976) challenged psychology to examine its biases and to be more inclusive in its theories. Thirty years later, psychology, as a profession, is slowly moving to an understanding that much of the research and theories developed in the past 100 years were developed from a European American perspective. This perspective assumed that the psychology that explained the behavior of White men applied to everyone. This ethnocentric viewpoint assumed that the White male born and raised in the United States represented the entire world. When one realizes that White men born in the United States represent slightly more than 100 million boys and men and the world's population is approximately 6.5 billion people, one can begin to see the absurdity of this claim. As we note in chapters 2, 3, and 6, the past 3 decades have shown psychologists that although there are some universal constructs, gender and race influence many constructs, and sexism and racism play a role in the psychology of people who are not White, as well as those who are White. Thus, it is important for psychologists to understand the role of culture in people's lives to truly understand their behavior.

We believe that psychologists are eager to strive to become culturally oriented. The "Guidelines on Multicultural Education, Training, Research, Practice, and Organizational Change for Psychologists," recently approved by the APA (2003; see also APA Web site version at http://www.apa.org/pi/multiculturalguidelines/), were written to help psychologists to become culturally centered in their work in education, training, research, practice, and organizational change. However, although the Guidelines provide a written guide of ways to become culturally oriented, they will help no one if they are not implemented. Our purpose in writing this book was to help psychologists gain a better understanding of the practical implications of the Guidelines in their work. In other words, we hope to help psychologists (a) know how to develop a better awareness of themselves and others and (b) learn what exactly the critical elements of a culturally centered educational program are and practical ways to become more culturally oriented as practitioners, researchers, and change agents. See Exhibit 1.1 for a preliminary self-assessment that psychologists can take as they begin this process. Our intended audience is psychologists who are educators, practitioners, researchers, and administrators, to help them know how to apply the Guidelines in their work.

This chapter discusses the demographic changes in the United States today, and the implications of those changes for psychology. We then provide some background of the development of the Guidelines as an attempt to help psychologists address the challenges of working with an increasingly diverse population. This chapter also includes definitions of terms used throughout the book, including *culture, culture-centered, multiculturalism, race,* and *ethnicity.* Finally, we provide an overview of the rest of the book.

Self-Assessment of Multicultural Awareness

- What is my cultural competence to this point?
- What are my perceptions of ethnoracially diverse groups? How were those perceptions developed?
- How have I tried to infuse cultural competence into my work as a psychologist or psychologist in training?
- Where do I need to grow most?
- How do I feel about this process? Am I scared, excited, angry, resistant?
- How can I find a way to be honest with myself?
- What is my goal in becoming a culturally competent psychologist?

Demographic Changes

In 2004, about 67% of the population identified as White, non-Hispanic (U.S. Census Bureau, 2004). Of the remaining individuals who identified as a member of an ethnoracial group, approximately 12% indicated they were African American; 1%, American Indian or Alaskan Native; 5%, Asian/Pacific Islander; 14%, Hispanic; and about 7% indicated some other race. These categories overlap, because individuals were able to choose more than one racial affiliation. Since the 2000 Census, the largest growth has been in the Hispanic and Asian American populations. For the first time, in 2003, the Hispanic ethnic group surpassed African Americans as the largest ethnoracial minority in the country.

As one might expect, ethnoracial diversity varies greatly by region of the country. M. B. Brewer and Suchan summarized the growth in diversity by region in a series of maps (2001). Those states with the most diversity (those with some counties that have 60%–77% ethnoracial minority groups) tend to be on the Atlantic or Pacific coasts or on the border with Mexico. These states include California, Texas, Arizona, New Mexico, and Virginia. States with medium to high diversity (counties with 49%–59% ethnoracial minority groups) are found across the country, however, and include Maryland, New York, Illinois, Washington State, Nevada, Colorado, Montana, Alaska, North Dakota, South Dakota, Minnesota, Wisconsin, Michigan, Arkansas, Louisiana, Alabama, and North and South Carolina. In addition, all states had some growth in diversity. Thus, even those psychologists working in the middle of the country in states that had previously been fairly homogeneously White will encounter ethnoracially diverse individuals.

Implications for Psychology

In 2001, the Surgeon General of the United States released a supplement to his 1999 study of the mental health system in the United States (U.S. Department of Health and Human Services [USDHHS], 1999, 2001). The introduction points to a stark and disturbing implication of the increasing diversity of the United States for psychologists, noting the

> existence of striking disparities for minorities in mental health services and the underlying knowledge base. Racial and ethnic minorities have less access to mental health services than do whites. They are less likely to receive needed care. When they receive care, it is more likely to be poor in quality. (USDHHS, 2001, p. 3)

In other words, ethnoracial individuals are not seeking treatment, staying in treatment, or receiving good quality treatment. The USDHHS report provides a powerful analysis of the need for mental health treatment for ethnoracial individuals, particularly documenting the burden of those needs in overall productivity and health. What is less clear is the reason for those unmet mental health needs, although one reason seems to be barriers due to practitioners' lack of cultural awareness and their culturally insensitive treatments. As the population of the United States is increasingly composed of individuals from racial/ethnic minority groups, the need for culturally sensitive treatments is going to become more imperative, both in the delivery of services and in developing empirically supported effective treatments across populations. Psychologists as practitioners and researchers must become more culturally oriented to be effective.

Particularly relevant to psychologists in institutions of higher education are ethnoracial differences in birth rates, such that professors can expect greater numbers of ethnoracially diverse students in their classrooms. Although college completion rates differed among Whites and ethnoracial minority students, ethnoracial minority students have increased their college attendance overall. When examining ethnoracial identities of those enrolled in college, researchers found that 68% were White, 12% were African American, 10% were Hispanic, 1% were American Indian, and 6% were Asian. This is roughly proportional to the representation of these groups in the population, with the exception of the Hispanic group. However, college completion differs by race/ethnicity. Statistics from the National Center on Education Statistics (2003) also show that 18.0% of White individuals had received a bachelor's degree, compared with 12.2% of African Americans, 25.0% of Asian/Pacific Islander Americans, 8.0% of American Indians, and 8.3% of Hispanics.

We examined the attainment of various types of degrees in psychology. The National Center on Educational Statistics indicated that in 2002, 76,670 bachelor's degrees were awarded in psychology; 14,888 master's degrees were awarded in psychology; and 4,341 doctoral degrees were awarded in psychology. Of those degrees, the majority were awarded to Whites (73% of bachelor's degrees, 75% of master's degrees, and 80% of doctoral degrees). African Americans received 11% of bachelor's degrees and 12% of master's degrees, equal to their representation in the population, but they were awarded only 6% of doctoral degrees. Other racial/ethnic groups were less well represented: Hispanics received 8% of bachelor's degrees and 6% of both master's and doctoral degrees in psychology; Asian/Pacific Islanders received 6% of bachelor's degrees in psychology and 4% of master's and doctoral degrees in psychology; and American Indians received less than 1% of all the degrees in psychology, with only 28 doctorates in psychology awarded to American Indians in 2002 (latest data available). Thus, for all but African Americans, ethnoracial minority students are underrepresented at all levels of psychology, but the need to increase minority representation is particularly critical at the doctoral level, because it is the primary entry point to become a psychologist.

Ethnoracial minority students appear to progressively drop out of the pipeline to become psychologists; their decisions may be due to personal or environmental reasons (e.g., discrimination and barriers due to external constraints). Ethnoracial representation among psychologists is also small. Kite et al.'s (2001) analysis of psychologists in academia noted that the numbers of ethnoracial minority psychologists were so small that they could not separate them by ethnicity. Indeed, in 2002, APA membership data indicated that 0.3% of the membership were American Indian, 1.7% were Asian, 2.1% were Hispanic, and 1.7% were African American (APA Research Office, 2002a), clearly delineating the serious underrepresentation of psychologists of color within the organization. Representation was slightly better within APA governance in 2002—1.7% were American Indian, 3.6% were Asian, 5.1% were African American, and 4.8% were Hispanic (APA Research Office, 2002b).

Background of the "Guidelines on Multicultural Education, Training, Research, Practice, and Organizational Change for Psychologists"

The need for psychologists, particularly practitioners, to develop competence to work with ethnoracial individuals has been a focus of several individuals and organizations for several decades. In 1981, then-president of APA Division 17 (Society of Counseling Psychology) Allen Ivey appointed Derald Sue to chair a task force to develop cross-cultural counseling competencies. The report of the task force was published in 1982 and outlined 11 competencies in the areas of awareness, knowledge, and skills. Those original 11 competencies were never formally endorsed by Division 17 nor by APA. However, Sue began to work with members of the American Counseling Association, and in 1992, Sue, Arredondo, and McDavis published an expanded version of the cross-cultural competencies. These 31 competencies were still organized around awareness, knowledge, and skills, but the writing team added the dimensions of self, other, and interventions, resulting in nine dimensions (e.g., awareness of self, knowledge of others, skills in interventions).

In the early 1990s, a number of individuals sought to bring the competencies back into APA, seeking formal approval of the competencies as APA policy. A special interest group within Division 17 was formed; their work culminated in a book published in 1998 (D. Sue et al., 1998) focusing on further defining the competencies in practice. Simultaneously, the presidents of Divisions 17, 35 (Society for the Psychology of Women), and 45 (Society for the Psychological Study of Ethnic Minority Issues) appointed a writing team to develop a document that would address competencies applied to education, training, practice, and research. We became cochairs of that writing team, shepherding the document through several iterations and revisions through a 4-year process. We represent the collective efforts of a number of individuals, including members of Divisions 17, 35, 45, as well as past presidents of APA and a working group convened jointly by the APA Board for the Advancement of Psychology in the Public Interest and the APA Board of Professional Affairs.

The APA Council of Representatives approved the Guidelines on August 21, 2002; they were published in the *American Psychologist* in May 2003. These Guidelines are broad and apply to all areas of psychology, as evidenced by the extensive and well-referenced document that went through a developmental and approval process that included all divisions, state associations, and APA boards and committees. The Guidelines, written in aspirational language, serve as a blueprint for professional psychologists. As noted previously, the final version of this document was strongly influenced by the contributions of a working group jointly convened by the APA Board for the Advancement of Psychology in the Public Interest and the APA Board of Professional Affairs.

We learned through our work as cochairs of the writing team for the Guidelines that psychologists are quite eager to take a culture-centered perspective but feel that they do not always know how to do that. Our aim is to provide concrete, specific examples to aid psychologists in the variety of settings in which they work.

The Theoretical and Empirical Basis for the Book

As we have noted, changing demographics in the United States indicate that all psychologists in all states are more likely to encounter individuals of different cultures in their work. But, at the same time, empirical research that documents ineffective treatments for some populations demonstrates a need for culture-centered psychology. As stated in the 2003 *American Psychologist* article,

> The "Guidelines on Multicultural Education, Training, Research, Practice, and Organizational Change for Psychologists" reflect the continuing evolution of the study of psychology, changes in society at large, and emerging data about the different needs of particular individuals and groups historically marginalized or disenfranchised within and by psychology on the basis of their ethnic/racial heritage and social group identity or membership. These "Guidelines on Multicultural Education, Training, Research, Practice, and Organizational Change for Psychologists" reflect knowledge and skills needed for the profession in the midst of dramatic historic sociopolitical changes in U.S. society, as well as needs from new constituencies, markets, and clients. (p. 377)

The 2003 article further discusses the Guidelines as being based on

> research, professional consensus, and literature addressing perceptions of ethnic minority groups and intergroup relationships (Dovidio & Gaertner, 1998; Dovidio, Gaertner, & Validzic, 1998; Gaertner & Dovidio, 2000), experiences of ethnic and racial minority groups (S. Sue, 1999; Swim & Stangor, 1998; USDHHS, 2000, 2001), multidisciplinary theoretical models about worldviews and identity (Arredondo & Glauner, 1992; Helms, 1990; Hostede, 1980; Kluckhohn & Strodbeck, 1961; Markus & Kitayama, 2001; D. W. Sue & Sue, 1977), and the work on cross-cultural and multicultural guidelines and competencies developed over the past 20 years (Arredondo et al., 1996; D. W. Sue, Arredondo, & McDavis, 1992; D. W. Sue et al., 1982). (p. 379)

In this book, we build on the empirical research cited in the Guidelines, updating that literature base and also providing concrete examples and case vignettes to help psychologists increase their multicultural competence as educators, researchers, and practitioners (Guidelines 3–5). Psychologists may also serve as agents of change in an increasingly multicultural society (Guideline 6). The latter, we believe, is critical, because although many psychologists are prepared as clinicians, facilitating individual and group-level change and development, there exist many needs for culturally effective psychologists at institutional and organizational levels. Already, multicultural organizational development and cultural competency development in health care and educational institutions are high priorities. Through multicultural-centered consultation and human behavior expertise, psychologists can facilitate relevance and responsiveness of training programs, human service agencies, and other organizations.

DEFINITIONS

We use in this book the same definitions used in the Guidelines (APA, 2003).

Culture

This term is defined as "the belief systems and value orientations that influence customs, norms, practices, and social institutions, including psychological processes (language, caretaking practices, media, educational systems) and organizations" (APA, 2003, p. 380). We begin with an assumption that everyone has a culture with an ethnoracial–cultural heritage, even though many White individuals have not identified themselves as members of a cultural group. *Culture* has been viewed as the way that a group has learned how to solve the problems of survival, raise children, and create order in their group. Individuals' worldviews (or the way they have learned to view the world) are shaped by their culture. Culture is not static; rather, it is fluid and dynamic. Some aspects of behavior are universal, spanning across all cultures (e.g., incest is taboo in all cultures); other aspects of behavior are culture specific.

Race

We define *race* as "the category to which others assign individuals on the basis of physical characteristics, such as skin color or hair type, and the generalizations and stereotypes made as a result" (APA, 2003, p. 380). The construct of "race" has a long and very heated history in the United States. The controversy includes the definition of *race* as biological or socially determined. Genotypic differences among racial groups do exist, but in reality the races in the world have become intermingled enough that any one individual is a mixture of many "races," although physical characteristics of one race may predominate in that individual. However, although researchers may suggest that biologically based racial differences are nonexistent, clearly the social construction of race has strong implications for individuals in the United States.

Ethnicity

We define *ethnicity* as "the acceptance of the group mores and practices of one's culture of origin and the concomitant sense of belonging" (APA, 2003, p. 380). Individuals may have many ethnic identities; some may be more salient at one time than another.

Multiculturalism

This term encompasses the concept of all the dimensions of identity on which individuals differ, including "race, ethnicity, language, sexual orientation, gender, age, disability, class status, education, religious/spiritual orientation, and other cultural dimensions" (APA, 2003, p. 380).

Diversity

The term *diversity* is used to refer to cultural and racial variation among individuals who are of European American, African American, Latino/Hispanic, Asian American, or Native American descent.

Culture-Centered

We frequently use the term *culture-centered* throughout the book. We use this term to encourage psychologists to use a cultural perspective, or "lens," as a way to interpret individuals' behavior: "In culture-centered practices, psychologists recognize that all individuals including themselves are influenced by different contexts, including the historical, ecological, sociopolitical, and disciplinary" (APA, 2003, p. 380).

CHAPTER OVERVIEWS

Each of the rest of the chapters in this book follows a similar format. At the beginning of each chapter, there are competency statements, followed by an overview of the chapter. Each chapter also provides activities and case vignettes to stimulate the readers' thinking and to provide material for discussion. We anticipate that this approach will assist instructors and readers alike by creating chapters that are user friendly.

In chapter 2 ("Evaluating Cultural Identity and Biases"), we discuss psychologists within their cultural context and how their perspectives are shaped by that culture. We first discuss the construct of "worldview" and how worldview differs across cultures and the profession of psychology. We then draw on the social psychological literature on social categorization theory to describe how individuals tend to view members of their "in-group" as positive and members of the "out-group" as negative. We encourage psychologists to become aware of their worldviews and the implicit stereotypes they may hold of other groups. We use a variety of exercises, case studies, and examples to help psychologists to increase their knowledge of themselves as cultural beings.

In chapter 3 ("Psychologists in Cross-Cultural Interactions With Others"), we discuss how important it is for psychologists to understand cultural perspectives of others. We discuss racial identity development models, the findings from social psychology about attribution errors made about other groups (devaluing other groups while valuing own group), and the recent literature on the effects of being a member of a stigmatized group. Research findings based on the constructs of "stereotype threat" and "tokenism" are introduced. We discuss the implications of these findings on behavior for clients, students, and colleagues. We encourage psychologists to become familiar with literature and theories related to specific racial/cultural groups, and we provide specific ways that psychologists may do this through case studies, exercises, and additional readings.

Chapter 4 ("Implications for Psychologists as Practitioners") addresses Guideline 5, focusing on psychologists as clinicians working with an increasingly diverse client population. The U.S. Surgeon General's report, *Mental Health: Culture, Race, and Ethnicity* (USDHHS, 2001), provides a compelling rationale for psychologists to become culturally sensitive and competent. If we do not, we will continue to underserve clients of color, run the risk of not providing appropriate treatment, and in some cases, have the potential to do harm to those seeking help. The Guidelines address three critical areas for clinicians: setting the clients' concerns and counseling goals within their cultural contexts, practicing culturally appropriate assessment techniques, and having a wide variety of intervention tools to use with varying client populations. This chapter provides psychologists with case studies, checklists, and exercises to help increase cultural competence as practitioners.

In chapter 5 ("Implications for Psychologists as Educators"), we discuss a rationale for a multicultural-centered approach to psychological education and training. We apply the material discussed in chapters 2 and 3 to two major areas: (a) fostering a multicultural-centered approach to teaching and (b) infusing a culture-centered perspective in psychological curricula and didactic courses across psychology; the latter also includes a focus on multicultural-centered clinical training.

In the first area, we discuss how different worldviews may influence students' approach to learning and interactions with faculty members. In the second area, we encourage faculty to infuse a multicultural-centered perspective into all courses. For example, the history of psychology would include the way that psychology has treated individuals of color and the reactions of ethnic minority psychologists over the years. We give examples of ways to infuse a multicultural-centered perspective into the curriculum in various areas of psychology. This chapter includes strategies for each of the areas listed previously, along with strategies to address students' resistance to a multicultural-centered approach.

The demographic changes discussed in chapter 1 will have strong implications for psychologists as researchers. These are discussed in chapter 6 ("Implications for Psychologists as Researchers"), beginning with the history of the treatment of culture in psychological research and the potential damage that it has caused. We discuss the perception of cultural limitations of psychological research and ways that psychologists may begin to address this. We also discuss the need for a culture-centered approach to research, from the design of a study, to application of psychological assessment, through the analysis of data. We outline concerns with current practice in each of these stages and then specific recommendations and suggestions for each stage. Similar to our approach in other chapters, we develop case studies and checklists to help psychologists apply this knowledge.

Psychologists often work within organizations, in many cases as members of the organization, and in other cases as consultants to organizations. Chapter 7 ("Psychologists as Organizational Change Agents") focuses on ways that psychologists may use their knowledge as multicultural-centered professionals to become catalysts for change. The Guidelines emphasize helping psychologists to become social change agents to promote a multicultural-centered society and to promote a culture-centered perspective in their roles as organizational consultants. This chapter focuses on ways that psychologists may do that, including case studies, examples of specific techniques, and additional resources.

The final chapter ("Concluding Thoughts: Psychology as a Transformed Profession") provides our perspectives about the potential for the future of psychology, as it becomes a multicultural-centered profession. This chapter shapes our vision both for additional areas of growth for the profession as a whole and for specific steps we can take as psychologists and as an association of psychologists.

Summary

In this chapter, we provided a basic rationale for the Guidelines and an overview of the demographic changes in the United States. We have given the definitions of terms related to race, culture, and diversity that we use through the book, as well as an overview of the rest of the book. We very much hope that students and psychologists will enjoy the case vignettes and exercises, and more critically, we hope that we will help prompt some thinking, evaluating, and growth, as psychologists become more culturally competent.

Evaluating Cultural Identity and Biases | 2

Because I, a mestiza, continually walk out of one culture into another, because I am in all cultures at the same time.

—Anzaldúa, 1987, p. 87

Guideline 1: Professionals are encouraged to recognize that, as cultural beings, they may hold attitudes and beliefs that can detrimentally influence their perceptions of and interactions with individuals who are ethnically and racially different from themselves.[1]

Competency Statements

Psychologists committed to multicultural-centered practices will be able to

- articulate the role of cultural heritage for their own personal and professional development;
- discuss their worldview based on family socialization and other influences, including research and educational philosophy in psychology;
- describe their ethnic–racial identity development processes;
- recognize the effects of social categorization in interactions with others that result in prejudice, discrimination, and other forms of oppressive behavior;
- examine conscious and unconscious negative stereotypes toward ethnoracial minorities even though they consider themselves egalitarian;
- recognize the fallacy of the color-blind paradigm;

---

[1]Cited in "Guidelines on Multicultural Education, Training, Research, Practice, and Organizational Change for Psychologists," American Psychological Association (APA; 2003, p. 382; see also APA Web site version at http://www.apa.org/pi/multiculturalguidelines/).

- apply the dimensions of personal identity model (Arredondo & Glauner, 1992) to self-evaluate priorities, privileges, and power that one may or may not accrue, on the basis of different dimensions of personal identity;
- recognize that all individuals are cultural beings affected differently by their dimensions of personal identity and contextual factors including historical events, sociopolitical enablers and barriers, and economics; and
- identify their areas in need of improvement to become more culturally oriented.

Cultural Self-Awareness and Knowledge of Others

Cultural encapsulation is the term used by Gilbert Wrenn (1962) to describe the blinders of counselors and psychologists in a world of cultural diversity. The changing demographics in the United States and globally are brought to all of us in multiple media forms often reinforcing generalizations and stereotypes about cultural groups. As cultural beings, psychologists are not immune to negative portrayals. They have been socialized and shaped by mainstream cultural values that permeate throughout formal education and that are reinforced by seemingly normative political policies and laws and serve to define in-groups and out-groups in this country. Neutrality in psychology education, research, assessment, and practice has been challenged by the "Guidelines on Multicultural Education, Training, Research, Practice, and Organizational Change for Psychologists" (American Psychological Association [APA], 2003; see also APA Web site version at http://www.apa.org/pi/multiculturalguidelines/), multicultural counseling competencies (Arredondo et al., 1996; D. W. Sue, Arredondo, & McDavis, 1992; D. W. Sue et al., 1982), and culture-specific documents (APA,1990; Council of National Psychological Associations for the Advancement of Ethnic Minority Interests, 2000, 2003) outlining considerations with ethnoracial minorities in particular as well as with lesbian, gay, bisexual, and transgendered clients (APA, 2001). The common denominator among these documents is a focus on the imperative for psychologists' cultural preparedness in a culturally pluralistic society.

The multicultural counseling competencies (Arredondo et al., 1996; D. W. Sue et al., 1992), a springboard for the Guidelines, provide a tripartite model that includes cultural self-awareness, knowledge, and awareness of others' worldview, as well as the application of culturally synergistic interventions, research methodologies, and institutional practices. In this chapter, the focus is on the first two domains, which place the responsibility on the psychologist for knowing oneself and extending this learning to building knowledge about other cultural beings; the latter is discussed more fully in chapter 3. The dimensions of personal identity (DPI; Arredondo & Glauner, 1992; see Figure 2.1) is used as the reference point for this personal examination. It is in this self-exploration that the recognition of one's worldview as exemplified through beliefs, values, biases, assumptions, and privileges may begin to emerge, enabling us as psychologists to further understand how we interact with others from our worldview.

From social attribution theory and racial identity development models, one can see that self-perception and perceptions of others are often at variance because of group-level categorizations (Fiske, 1998; Steele, 1997; D. W. Sue & Sue, 2003). The DPI provides a mirror for self-assessment of identity factors that emerge at birth, external or contextual forces that influence one's worldview and life experiences, and the choices one makes based on birthright, opportunities, and access in a democratic society such as the United States. We describe the A and C Dimensions before the B Dimension.

The A Dimensions reflect items on an application form for credit or an intake form people complete at the physician's office. Although in the latter example, responding to these items may be optional, no one is exempt from possessing these A Dimensions. Most are acquired at birth. For some individuals, physicality or physical disabilities are lifelong dimensions, whereas others become disabled via an accident or another unexpected event or through the aging process. Social class is listed as an A Dimension because this is a birthright with both positive and negative consequences. In the United States, heritage deriving from the Mayflower settlers is deemed desirable, celebrating this through associations such as the Daughters of the American Revolution. Social categorization, particularly for White, heterosexual, formally educated men, attributes status and privilege (Fouad & Brown, 2000). Although high social status is not always a birthright for White men, it is definitely much less so for White women and for ethnoracial minorities of either gender. Our definition of *high social class* does not equate educational achievement with socioeconomic status, although there are data that indicate (a) that Latinos in the United States have greater limitations to access higher education than other cultural groups because of low family income and (b) that women who enter the faculty ranks are still paid less than their male counterparts. All psychologists possess A Dimensions and place differential value on them. For instance, a person may value his or her ethnic heritage, but others may attribute only negative stereotypes to this ethnic group. Some individuals may prioritize their gay or lesbian identity,

Figure 2.1. Dimensions of personal identity. Copyright 1992 P. Arredondo and T. Glauner, Empowerment Workshops, Inc. Reprinted with permission of the authors.

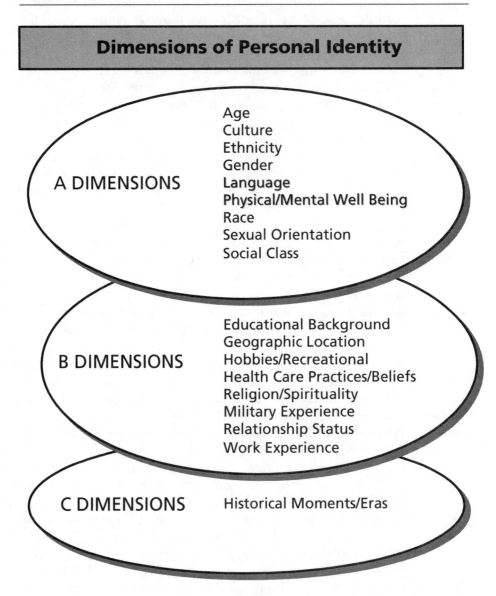

Dimensions of Personal Identity

A DIMENSIONS
Age
Culture
Ethnicity
Gender
Language
Physical/Mental Well Being
Race
Sexual Orientation
Social Class

B DIMENSIONS
Educational Background
Geographic Location
Hobbies/Recreational
Health Care Practices/Beliefs
Religion/Spirituality
Military Experience
Relationship Status
Work Experience

C DIMENSIONS
Historical Moments/Eras

whereas others may see them on the basis of their visible phenotype (e.g., Asians or African Americans). Janet Helms (1984) has coined the term *visible ethnic racial group* in reference to ethnoracial minorities. The dimensions can be placed on a continuum with positive and negative poles based on personal and other attributions and perceptions, as illustrated in Exhibit 2.1.

EXHIBIT 2.1

Valuing of Dimensions of Personal Identity

Valuing of Dimensions of Personal Identity—Self-Appraisal

Ethnicity

Very important				Not that important
100	75	50	25	0
X				

Gender

Very important		Not that important
X		

Valuing of Dimensions of Personal Identity—Personal—Appraisal of Others

Ethnicity

Very important				Not that important
100	75	50	25	0
		X		

Gender

Very important		Not that important
		X

Stereotypes are readily formed about the A Dimensions leading to behaviors described in psychology as the "self-fulfilling prophecy," "learned helplessness" (Seligman, 1975), and "stereotype threat" (Steele, 1997). The latter construct describes an individual or group's performance to widely held societal stereotypes (e.g., girls are not suited for math and science, ethnoracial minorities score poorly on standardized tests). It is logical, therefore, for educators, clinicians, and researchers alike to review their beliefs about an individual's potential performance, communication, and so forth on the basis of A Dimensions.

Finally, many of the A Dimensions are protected by federal legislation. The Civil Rights Act of 1964 led to policies to protect minority identities based on birth—national origin, race, and gender—in employment, education, and housing. This landmark law led to the creation of Title IX (1972), for gender equity; sexual harassment laws; and the Americans With Disabilities Act of 1990. Laws to protect individuals on the basis of sexual orientation have been created at state and local levels.

The C Dimension introduces historical, familial, and ecological factors that affect life span development and other life opportunities. Arredondo and Glauner (1992) theorized that historical events such as the Depression, slavery, the Holocaust in Nazi Germany, the genocide of American Indians, colonization of Mexicans in the Southwest, and the terrorist attacks of September 11, 2001, leave legacies for those who lived through them and their descendants. Psychological memories persist across generations for families because of the horrors of these events. Immigration is another example of a historical moment. Most psychologists have immigrants in their ancestries, some more recent, and some may be immigrants themselves. The experience and processes of immigration are life altering, leading to physical, emotional, and spiritual changes. In effect, the C Dimension includes forces that one cannot control, such as wars, natural disasters, parent's divorce, economic recessions, and policies that repress basic rights and freedoms, such as with undocumented immigrants.

For psychologists working in clinical settings, consciousness of these ecological, sociopolitical, and historical forces cannot be minimized, because of the differential effects they have on individuals and groups, particularly historically marginalized groups. A vivid example lies with the survivors of Hurricane Katrina that slammed New Orleans and the Gulf Coast in August 2005. There was an overrepresentation of African Americans with fewer socioeconomic resources among the survivors. The media blitzed the public with images of families who had lost everything from family and friends to personal possessions. Unfortunately, the human interest stories were not well-balanced, leaving the general public with messages about downtrodden people still in shock and not enough about the inner fortitude and hope that was buoying them. When encountering individuals and families who have suffered life-threatening challenges, well-intentioned clinicians must evaluate their personal biases and assumptions about these clients in order to not patronize or see them from deficit perspectives.

The B Dimension is discussed last because Arredondo and Glauner (1992) posited that many of these dimensions are affected by the interaction of the A and C Dimensions of identity. Education, geographic location, relationship status, work experience, health care practices, and even religious and spiritual preferences are deemed to be changeable. More equitable access to higher education for ethnoracial minorities was achieved through the passage of the Civil Rights Act. The federal government's emphasis on promoting the sciences and engineering for women in higher education allowed more women entry into these predominantly male professions.

Education is perhaps the most catalytic variable among the B Dimensions, because of the possibilities that may result from educational attainment for work experience, geographical mobility, health care practices, or lack thereof. Many psychologists are privileged as a result of degrees earned, the nationally ranked program attended, and one's specialty area, and this privilege interacts with the A Dimensions of ethnicity and gender in particular. For example, although it is not publicly discussed, many ethnoracial minorities were historically discouraged from conducting research on topics of race, ethnic identity, immigration, and so forth because these were not perceived to fall under the purview of serious science. Rather than making assumptions, it is always necessary to notice individuals' A and B Dimensions and how these may be a barrier or an enabler to career advancement because of institutional racism.

The DPI suggests that psychologists examine how they arrived where they are and how their advantages or journeys may not be similar for other psychologists, on the basis of their A, B, and C Dimensions. The examples go beyond that of psychologists, to students, clients, peers, and others with whom we have contact. As educators, researchers, clinicians, and organizational administrators, we have to keep in mind that everyone has their DPI profile that makes them unique cultural beings with some shared group identities (see Exhibit 2.2).

Minority and Racial Cultural Identity Development

Implicit in this discussion of Guideline 1 is reference to minority and racial cultural identity development models (Atkinson, Morten, & Sue, 1989; Cross, 1991; Hardiman, 1982; Helms, 1990) and the concept of "White privilege" (McIntosh, 1989). Unlike the DPI, these are principally stage models, with movement through different stages or statuses precipitated by events that contribute to cognitive and emotional dissonance and then to changes in one's ethnic and racial identity status. To further recognize one's often-unconscious attitudes and beliefs across ethnic and racial differences, a personal examination of the models is recommended.

WHITE IDENTITY DEVELOPMENT MODELS

White identity development models have become an integral part of multicultural psychology coursework. Two theorists (Hardiman, 1982; Helms, 1990) of these models recognized that the majority of mental health professionals are White, making racial identity self-understanding an essential personal and professional development competency. Core to the developmental processes described by the theorists is the construct of "White privilege," as is discussed in the next subsection.

Directions: Identify 2–3 A and B Dimensions that are currently most salient for you and historical incidents that have impacted your personal development. Explain the rationale for the salience of these particular A and B Dimensions and discuss the influence of the A and C Dimensions on the B Dimensions.

Hardiman's (1982) White racial identity development model conceptualized five stages based on her study of biographies of White persons who she posited had achieved higher levels of racial consciousness. In brief, the stages are: (a) *naiveté*, or lack of social consciousness; (b) *acceptance*, symbolized by conscious egalitarianism or democratic ideals (Hardiman contends that acceptance may be a lifetime, enduring stage); (c) *resistance*, a transition stage involving questioning of White superiority and previous denial of racism; (d) *redefinition* of one's identity in relation to White privilege; and (e) *internalization* of new learning to form an evolved personal identity. Hardiman's model refers primarily to the A Dimensions of ethnicity and race as birthrights for White individuals in contrast to individuals of African heritage. In this regard, it is not inclusive of other ethnoracial minority groups or other dimensions of one's personal identity. Minimally, there is a reference to C Dimension events that may precipitate one's consciousness about discrimination in employment, education, or other human rights.

The Helms (1984, 1990) White racial identity model has evolved over time to include an assessment instrument (Parham & Helms, 1985) and to become the most discussed White identity development model in psychology. Helms has proposed two phases involving six statuses that lead to the development of a healthy White identity. The two phases are (a) abandonment of racism and (b) defining a nonracist White identity. Implicit in this process is the use of defenses or what Helms (1995) refers to as "information processing strategies" (IPSs). The IPSs refer to the emotional components of each status necessary to manage one's discomfort with the topic of race.

The statuses and IPSs are as follows: (a) *contact status*, obliviousness or denial of being racist; (b) *disintegration status*, suppression and ambivalence about being racist; (c) *reintegration status*, displacement and distortion of the out-group; (d) *pseudoindependence status*, selective perception of others and reshaping realities; (e) *immersion–emersion status*, more reshaping and hypervigilance about benefits of White privilege; and (f) *autonomy status*, enhanced cognitive flexibility (D. W. Sue & Sue, 2003). The Helms (1984, 1990) model, similar to that of Hardiman (1982), discusses White identity in the context of the "Other" being of African heritage. However, with the increase of more visible ethnic racial groups in the United States, the interpersonal processes Helms has outlined may likely apply to contact between Whites and Latinos, Asians, and American Indians.

WHITE PRIVILEGE

"White privilege," a construct implicit in both models of White identity development, gained popularity with "White Privilege: Unpacking the Invisible Knapsack" (McIntosh, 1989). The premise of this widely quoted article is that being White is a birthright in the United States that affords individuals benefits and privileges that they do not have to think about when they seek credit, shop for a car, decide to buy a house in a particular neighborhood, or go through airport security. In other words, Whiteness endows these individuals certain "unalienable rights" just because they are White. Moreover, McIntosh (1989) indicates that White people take these privileges for granted—Life is this way and questioning of one's place is not necessary. It's as if Whites say, "I can, if I wish, arrange to be in the company of people of my race most of the time" (McIntosh, 1989, p. 10).

Theorizing and living Whiteness and White politics were among the themes discussed in *Off White: Readings on Race, Power, and Society* (Fine, Weis, Powell, & Wong, 1997). A number of writers gave their voices to this edited volume of essays that position "Whiteness front and center of the analysis in order to subject it to the kind of scrutiny that rouses it off of unmarked space" (p. viii). Consistent with McIntosh's (1989) premises, the authors indicated that "Whiteness defines social identities and cross-racial relations as profoundly as it is denied" (p. x).

"White privilege" refers principally to individuals of European American heritage. Although others may "pass" because of their visible Whiteness, there may be differential treatment because of Middle Eastern, East Asian, or Jewish heritage. Another limitation to the "White privilege" concept is socioeconomic status. The opportunities of poor Whites contrast with those of higher socioeconomic status, as often these individuals are assigned an out-group status.

MINORITY IDENTITY DEVELOPMENT MODELS

The minority identity development model (Atkinson et al., 1989), renamed the racial–cultural identity development model (RCID; Atkinson, Morten, & Sue, 1998) grew out of the early work of William Cross, who focused on Black identity development. RCID offers a multidimensional, stage process that applies to ethnoracial minorities or to individuals who consider themselves members of a marginalized group on the basis of various A Dimensions (e.g., age, disability, sexual orientation). The precipitators for the development of a sense of minority identity are described as oppression and discrimination, and the five emergent stages are conformity, dissonance and appreciation, resistance and immersion, introspection, and integrative awareness. At each stage, individuals also have comparative or evaluative experiences along four dimensions: attitude toward self, attitude toward others of the same minority group, attitude toward others of a different minority group, and attitude toward dominant group.

The RCID model can be helpful in understanding the attitudes of students, clients, and colleagues who may seem to be very negative or highly ethnocentric about their ethnic identity. In such an analysis, one would begin at the first stage of *conformity*. For example, a Vietnamese teenager may feel unhappy with her racial identity, loathing of others who share her racial identity, discriminatory toward other ethnoracial minorities, and idealizing the White dominant group. Another example may lie with a graduate student who strongly aligns with his ethnoracial heritage and is critical of the benefits of White privilege and historical discriminatory laws against ethnic minorities. This person would be positioned in the *resistance and immersion* stage. It is also possible for an immigrant, professional adult with an intact sense of cultural identity to arrive in the United States at the stage of *integrative awareness*. After being denied work opportunities because of language difficulties and nonrecognition of his or her professional credentials, the immigrant may slip into the *resistance and immersion* stage, with feelings of depreciation for the dominant group.

The RCID may also apply to other groups that have been marginalized because of religious affiliation, sexual orientation, physical disability, and so forth. White gay men who decide to declare their homosexual identity may find that their seeming privileged status as White men is lost because they are now oppressed for their gay minority identity. Similar to the DPI, the RCID is contextual, reflecting individuals' cognitive and emotional dissonance based on external forces that cannot be controlled (e.g., discrimination in the workplace, living in segregated neighborhoods).

Implications of Self-Appraisal

Psychologists as educators, researchers, and practitioners can readily apply the RCID or one of the White identity development models to their own cultural identity development experiences. By so doing, they may be able to consciously determine unresolved attitudes and beliefs toward their own cultural heritage; for instance, they may ask themselves, Do I still resent persons of color who I believe have "benefited" from affirmative action? Do I believe that attending to cultural factors when conducting research is a waste of time because research is unbiased science? Do I believe that White superiority is a fact? Do I claim that I am color blind, that I see everyone as the same? If they answer Yes to any of these questions and they are White, they are expressing White privilege. If they answer Yes and are a member of an ethnoracial minority group, they may be in the conformity stage of the RCID.

Raising awareness also requires specific behaviors that psychologists may apply. Consider these statements: Culturally skilled psychologists "appreciate and articulate positive aspects of their own heritage that provide them with strengths in understanding differences"; "can recognize specific attitudes, beliefs and values from their own heritage and cultural learning that support behaviors that demonstrate respect and valuing of differences and those that impede or hinder respect and valuing of differences" (Arredondo et al., 1996, p. 57).

Considerations About Emotions

The role of emotions in recognizing attitudes and beliefs about one's cultural heritage and in relationships with ethnoracial minorities is a critical dimension of Guideline 1. Helms (1990) refers to some cognitive emotional defenses (e.g., ambivalence, hypervigilance) by connecting IPSs to the six statuses of White identity development (as we discussed previously). There are a range of emotions that emerge when students and professionals are asked to examine their cultural heritage; their role in neglecting ethnicity, race, and culture in psychology; and their responsibility to dismantle forms of institutional oppression. It is in the teaching of multicultural psychology where evidence emerges for the strengths and use of personal emotions, particularly defense mechanisms.

Defense Mechanisms

Participation in multicultural psychology or counseling training often precipitates unexpected feelings because, unlike other academic coursework, multicultural counseling introduces topics that become personalized. Students typically describe initial feelings of shock and dismay because they do not want to accept what they have read in the textbook. It is not unusual for students to criticize the textbook authors and blame them for promoting prejudice against White people. For many White students, feelings of denial, frustration, guilt, shame, and anger are expressed as they realize that they can no longer deny their White privilege.

For individuals who have grown up with the impression that they are not racist (Hardiman, 1982), course readings and assignments may introduce for the first time shared or unfamiliar life experiences based on different dimensions of personal identity. Assumptions about fairness and equality under the law may come into question as one reads case examples about institutional racism. Defense mechanisms of denial, displacement, blame, projection, and reaction formation are often voiced in response to reading assignments and through group discussions. Individuals may express beliefs that laws to protect ethnoracial minorities are sufficient and that hard work is the key to advancement. In other words, they subscribe to paradigms of meritocracy and color blindness (Wolsko, Park, Judd, & Wittenbrink, 2000), denying the continuation of institutional racism and blaming ethnoracial minorities for having unfair advantage over Whites, particularly in education and employment. These assertions are made without factual evidence but are held as beliefs because of what has been reported in the media, in textbooks, and by political figures.

The individuals most at risk in a multicultural psychology course or continuing education workshop are the instructors. More typically, these instructors are men and women of color and White women. In a university setting, they tend to be junior or adjunct faculty, often affecting attributions of respect and credibility. Anecdotal reports indicate that when students' personal beliefs are questioned, feelings of anger and frustration are often displaced, with the instructor becoming the scapegoat. Critiques of the textbook and references to exemplary individuals of color who have "made it" on the basis of their hard work are often voiced as a means of challenging the instructor.

Intellectualization is perhaps the most protective defense mechanism used by professionals to mask their emotions about multicultural issues. Because of training as scientists, evidence is often sought to explain disparities to equal opportunity to education, health care, and other services persons of privilege taken for granted. Minimization of the importance of multicultural competency development is often voiced in the name of equal treatment of all people. In these discussions, affect is noteworthy. Individuals who feel passionate about the color-blind paradigm and equality for all and believe in their nonracist attitudes often argue with conviction about their beliefs, seemingly attempting to convince others to believe them.

Defense mechanisms also emerge in clinical practice and supervision. Interns who may have had strong and positive experience with multicultural psychology may find themselves in supervision with a culturally encapsulated person. The power differential between supervisor and intern may further exacerbate the dissonance the intern feels because his or her concerns about the psychological effects of racism and sexism for a client are minimized by the supervisor. Conversely, a supervisor of color who emphasizes the role of context and family relations for

EXHIBIT 2.3

Your Own Emotions

When you learned that your program of study was requiring multicultural coursework, how did you feel? Happy, sad, satisfied, disappointed?

When you read the Surgeon General's report (U.S. Department of Health and Human Services, 2001) about disparities in health and mental health care for ethnoracial minorities, how did you feel? Upset and angry because your research agenda was not going to be a federal priority? Validated and satisfied because you knew this to be a fact based on findings from your work with community mental health agencies?

If you are conducting a study and federal agencies insist that you explain the cultural diversity of the populations in your study, how do you feel?

When you learned that the APA Council of Representatives had endorsed the "Guidelines on Multicultural Education and Training, Research, Practice, and Organization Change for Psychologists" how did you feel? Relieved, because now you did not have to be the only voice advocating for multicultural competency? Disgusted, because you believe that the guidelines are a waste time in scientific endeavors? Concerned, because now you might have to behave differently?

---

clients of color may be challenged by the supervisee who believes that individuals are responsible for their emotional well-being and that societal forces affect everyone equally.

Addressing Guideline 1 requires a discussion of emotions because examination of attitudes, beliefs, and perceptions and reflecting on interactions with others who are culturally different from oneself are highly personal. Furthermore, confronting personal defenses is particularly challenging for helping professionals because of the personal motivation that leads most of us to these careers. We psychologists like to believe that we are fair-minded and social justice oriented individuals who are trying to advance knowledge through teaching and research and to make a difference in someone's life through clinical practice. Recognition of different realities in a democratic society because of ethnoracial and socioeconomic differences can become a turning point in one's cultural identity development. Cognitive and emotional dissonance can facilitate one's commitment to be a more culturally competent professional. Balancing the dissonant feelings are hopefulness, encouragement that one is not alone in the journey of cultural competence development, and even excitement that one can become active in making changes to the discipline of psychology (see Exhibit 2.3).

Relevant Social Learning Constructs

Social learning theory provides a body of knowledge about learned behavior from society at large, from personal contact, and from academic study that influences one's worldview (beliefs, values, biases and assumptions, emotions, and behaviors). The enactment of Guideline 1 can be furthered by social learning theory constructs, helpful for understanding the role of emotions in relation to self and others, learned behavior that influences self-identity, self and social categorizations, prejudice, and stereotyping. There are multiple models and theories for conceptualizing the continuum of social identity to personal identity, such as self-categorization theory, boundaries of self, emotional bases of identity, and the formulation of in-group and out-group analyses that leads to behavioral practices (Harré & Moghaddam, 2003). Although all of these constructs are a field of study unto themselves, they relate to Guideline 1 and recognition of "attitudes and beliefs that can detrimentally influence their [psychologists'] perceptions of and interactions" (APA, 2003, p. 382) of others. A brief discussion of several constructs follows.

Categorization

The previous discussions about the DPI suggest that self- and other categorization is a cognitive process in which all persons participate. Why do people categorize? First, it is important to realize that categorization is a learned response, often automatic and outside of one's conscious processing. Consider some of the reasons for categorization. It (a) is an efficient way to organize overwhelming information in interactions (e.g., "This woman speaks with such a thick accent, she will be a tough client"); (b) reduces information into manageable chunks that go together (e.g., "These are all poor families, education is not a priority for them"); (c) leads to associating various traits and behaviors with particular groups, even if they are inaccurate for particular, many, or even most individuals (e.g., "All American Indians prefer to live on reservations"); and (d) allows people to place value: In-groups are viewed favorably, highly valued, more trusted, and perceived as more cooperative and out-groups are viewed homogeneously and negatively.

Stereotyping: A Form of Categorization

Stereotypes, generally speaking, are negative attributions or forms of devaluation of others. They are perceptions and assumptions about an individual or individuals on the basis of group affiliation. The earlier discussion of A Dimensions is relevant here because nearly all of these immutable dimensions are readily stereotyped. One can argue that at face value, stereotyping is not harmful because it is a shortcut to make assumptions or engage a mental mind-set about a group member. However, when stereotypes are used to make judgments about employment, a client's ability to pay, or a clinical diagnosis, biases or prejudices take

Influence of the Media

The media is the primary communicator of stereotypes. Consider the following: (a) How often are people with similar A Dimensions to yours negatively stereotyped in print media, on television, on talk radio? (b) With which groups do you self-categorize and why? (c) How have stereotypes adversely affected you personally and professionally?

over. The result is discriminatory behavior with adverse consequences for the individual.

No one, including psychologists, is immune to stereotyping, because of the early onset of learning about stereotypes and their reinforcement by the media (see Exhibit 2.4). The famous doll study (Clark & Clark, 1947) revealed the preference by Black children of White dolls, indicating that children learn as early as age 3 to devalue people with dark skin (Crocker, Major, & Steele, 1998). Other reports indicate that "stereotypes about homosexuals are also learned early in life" (Crocker et al., 1998, p. 511). Quite often, stereotypes are assumed to be facts and accepted as the truth about one individual and generalized to others who share the same group identity (e.g., immigrants). Anti-immigrant stereotypes suggest that these individuals are using public assistance and other services that only tax-paying citizens deserve. Inflammatory messages can confuse even well-intentioned ethical psychologists. The human challenge is that until a stereotype is disconfirmed, it remains a fact. Even those who consciously hold egalitarian beliefs may hold unconscious endorsement of negative attitudes about ethnoracial minority groups (i.e., immigrants are on public assistance and unwilling to learn English).

Self-Categorization

The theory of optimal distinctiveness, a form of self-categorization theory, suggests that there is a point along a continuum that optimally satisfies a person's need for identity. That is, individuals strive to be different from others while sharing a sense of similarity to others that is balanced. The ability to perceive one's identity groups (e.g., ethnic, sexual orientation) as distinctive and well-regarded in comparison to other groups will bolster one's sense of both distinctiveness and belonging (M. B. Brewer, 1991). However, Allport (1954) indicated that "attachment to one's in-group does not necessarily require hostility toward out-groups" (as cited in M. B. Brewer, 1999, p. 429). As ethnic minority women, we have often felt a greater sense of connection in the company of other ethnoracial minority women, but this does not mean that we hold disdain for White women and men. Even more specifically, one of us (Patricia Arredondo), might consider her specific affinity to Latino psychologists as an example of ethnocentrism because of the sense of belonging she feels based on their shared histories, cultural values, and so forth. Self-categorization may serve different purposes—to feel special, to distance oneself, and to have the flexibility when to engage and with whom.

In the profession of psychology, populated primarily by White psychologists, presumably it would be easier for Whites to experience a sense of belonging at APA conferences, in graduate training programs, and where one is employed. McIntosh's (1989) concept of "White privilege," the freedom to experience sameness because one is a White psychologist, may apply here. The facility to have social and personal identity affirmed, however, can lead to intergroup bias or ethnocentrism. Within APA and in other settings in which psychologists are employed or function professionally (e.g., state psychological associations), social categorization of in-groups and out-groups may de facto occur. For example, many state psychological associations have formed ethnic minority committees, a way to promote ethnoracial diversity membership. With the establishment of such committees, there may be an assumption on the part of the association's leadership that ethnoracial minority psychologists feel affirmed. This may be an accurate perception for some, but others may feel that they are relegated to an out-group status. Much depends on how ethnoracial minority task forces or committees within a majority White association are established, affirmed, and integrated into the entire organization. Power differentials are always in play, and this dynamic must be monitored even with well-intentioned group or category formation.

What might be some of the negative and positive effects of self-categorization? On one hand, it can be posited that because people are social beings, we all have needs for a sense of belonging, intergroup affiliations and recognition, and a shared identity. The same holds true for psychologists who may not always experience acceptance, fit, or validation in the majority contexts in which they must operate on a daily basis. Choosing to associate with other ethnic minority or women coworkers for lunch or other social events may give one the sense of belonging that otherwise is not validated at work. The same example can be extended to nonpsychologists who become clients, research participants, and students. Participants in research are often seen for only one to two A Dimensions that become variables in a study, whereas in reality the A Dimensions provide a strong sense of self-categorization.

The negative effects of self-categorization also need to be considered. Self-marginalization and the formation of special groups may serve the need of group members for self-preservation, validation, and promotion of shared interests and life histories. Ethnic minorities and women have formed special interest organizations in psychology and other fields and are often the focus of critical attributions by those who "do not belong." Some of the criticisms of self-categorization may be that group members are not being collegial, are discriminating, and simply not sharing. In short, there are two sides to the coin of self-categorization.

To summarize this discussion, the DPI is referenced once again because of the relevance it holds for self-categorization. Although the dimensions may not always be visible, culturally responsive psychologists are encouraged to (a) recognize that out-group status may be a daily occurrence for persons of color, regardless of their professional status; (b) determine where and with whom one feels affirmed personally; (c) identify emotional bases for identity (sources of comfort or discomfort); and (d) recognize one's privilege based on social categorization by others.

Positioning and the Emotions

Another relevant social learning construct is "positioning" (Apter, 2003). Primarily used in the field of consumer marketing, positioning is associated with motivational theory, suggesting that individuals turn their attention to what motivates them (products) and will satisfy their needs. As cultural beings, psychologists have been socialized to orient their attention to some individuals more than others. Positioning becomes a three-part process: (a) formulating categorization and self-categorization mindsets, (b) developing emotional responses that correspond to these categorizations, and (c) engaging or not engaging with others on the basis of positioning. For example, one of us (Patricia Arredondo) as a child was told that her neighbors on the right were proper people. They were White ethnics (English), were Protestants, retired, had a house on a corner lot and a nice yard and car, and basically kept to themselves (except for their barking dog). Her neighbors to the left were also White ethnics (Greek) but were immigrants. The grandfather tended to his garden; the mother took care of the two children and the home, and the father worked at the Ford plant. All spoke with an accent. At times, Patricia and her siblings were told to minimize their contact with the Greek family, primarily because the father screamed at the children for misbehaving; this was not proper behavior. They learned to position more positive emotions toward the older retired, quiet neighbors, because her mother esteemed them for being White Americans. Although she never developed negative emotions toward immigrants with accents (her father was an immigrant from Mexico), there were sufficient messages in the community encouraging her to turn away from those neighbors and others "like them." These strong social messages, however, did not take hold for her.

As Parrott (2003) stated, "Emotions play a central role in positioning" (p. 29), and according to researchers, empathy may facilitate changes in intergroup attitudes and behavior. There are two aspects to empathy: the cognitive aspect, which allows for role or perspective taking, and the emotional aspect, which reflects reactions to others. Information sharing, often described as "awareness building," may broaden psychologists' recognition about why students or employees of color prefer to sit together in the cafeteria. They may feel sad about the others' need to find comfort with others of the same ethnoracial group. However, intellectual empathy and a fleeting emotional reaction are insufficient for acceptance of another out-group such as African American teenage mothers or Latino gang members. When there is a habit of negative emotional positioning toward an ethnoracial minority group, it is not easy to break.

In the earlier discussion about White identity development, IPSs were identified as defenses to manage one's discomfort regarding the topic of race, prejudice, discrimination, and White privilege. For example, persons in the contact-status stage will likely continue to use defenses to reinforce negative positioning and limit their cross-cultural contacts, whereas those in the disintegration-status stage may find contact acceptable in neutral spaces such as the classroom. Individuals further along in their White identity development process will likely reduce negative positioning behavior. Those in the immersion–emersion status stage will be more hypervigilant about benefits of White privilege.

Roadblocks to Multicultural Self-Development

In the multicultural psychology literature, the concept of "worldview" is used to capture the composite of individuals' beliefs, values, traditions, and practices. The Kluckhohn and Kroeber (1963) model posits worldviews in five areas. One of the areas is orientation to human nature. According to the model, humans see others as basically good, basically bad, and basically good and bad (Kluckhohn & Kroeber, 1963). Psychologists would likely say that they see others as "basically good," an innocent-until-proven-guilty mind-set. However, this position may break down if one has not engaged in racial identity self-examination. For instance, the U.S. Supreme Court ruling on affirmative action (*Grutter v. Bollinger*, 2003) had many well-meaning academics agreeing with the decision that race should not be a factor in college admissions. We suggest that statements like this by psychologists and other well-intentioned professionals about meritocracy or leveling the playing field for everyone are simply strategies to deny that racism is still a problem in the United States.

Another roadblock is the color-blind approach, or the tendency to focus on universal human behavior. Statements such as "we all know the pain of death" or "we all bleed the same," regardless of color, attempt to minimize and deny ethnoracial differences. Social psychologists have found that "ignoring group differences often means that, by default, existing intergroup inequalities are perpetuated" (M. B. Brewer & Brown, 1998, p. 583).

Unintentional racism in counseling and psychotherapy has been discussed by C. R. Ridley (1995). He identifies seven racially related defenses that are precipitators of unintentional racist behavior. These are color blindness, color consciousness, cultural transference, cultural countertransference, cultural ambivalence, pseudotransference, and over-identification. With *color consciousness*, the therapist blames the client, indicating that problems are based on the client's ethnoracial identity. *Cultural countertransference* bears similarity to emotional positioning previously discussed. Here, the therapist reacts to the client because of previous encounters with others of the same ethnoracial minority background or in response to media portrayals. Assumptions are made without the basis of facts, and the assumptions can become facts for the therapist engaging in defensive cultural countertransference behaviors.

Resistance to change is often discussed in the multicultural psychology literature, although many professionals and students believe this area of study does not apply to them. Explanations of resistance are that multicultural psychology is the business of ethnoracial minority psychologists and students, that science is color blind, and that ethics prevent racism. Although the Guidelines apply to all psychologists, not all psychologists believe this is relevant to them.

Becoming a multiculturally competent psychologist requires an action orientation that is goal-oriented, developmental, and continuous. We culture-centered psychologists will readily admit that we are on a continuous learning curve, that we don't know it all, and that we also make cultural faux pas.

Summary

Culture is dynamic, and cultural differences are also dynamic. We psychologists, as cultural beings, can continue to evolve in our self-

EXHIBIT 2.5

Self-Evaluation

- About which ethnoracial minority group(s) do you stereotype most?
- When was the last time you applied the color-blind approach?
- What motivates attitude change for you, cognitive or emotional dissonance, or both?
- Which defenses do you typically use in interracial encounters?
- If you are White, how has "White privilege" benefited you?

understanding and understanding of others. To not do so willingly will surely cause frustration, errors, unintentional racism, and ethical malpractice. In closing this chapter, we raise several questions. Readers are encouraged to take the time to answer these as an opportunity to broaden cultural self-awareness in support of Guideline 1 (see Exhibit 2.5).

Psychologists in Cross-Cultural Interactions With Others

3

You can't shake hands with a closed fist.
—Indira Gandhi, quoted in Simpson, 1988, p. 5

Guideline 2: Psychologists are encouraged to recognize the importance of multicultural sensitivity/responsiveness, knowledge of, and understanding about ethnically and racially different individuals.[1]

Competency Statements

Psychologists committed to developing their interpersonal, multicultural competence in interactions will be able to articulate

- how their communication style (verbal and nonverbal) is influenced by perceptions of the "Other" and affects receivers of their message;
- how others' communication style (verbal and nonverbal) affects how they hear a message and the attributions they make to the speaker;
- high- and low-context communication from different cultural socialization;
- how the role of microaggressions, dynamics of power and White privilege, and aversive racism perpetuate intergroup bias; and
- how the contact hypothesis can contribute to more positive intergroup relations.

---

[1]Cited in "Guidelines on Multicultural Education, Training, Research, Practice, and Organizational Change for Psychologists," American Psychological Association (APA; 2003, p. 385; see also APA Web site version at http://www.apa.org/pi/multiculturalguidelines/).

Interacting Worldviews in Cross-Cultural Relationships

Historically, attention to ethnoracial minorities in psychology and to other minority groups involved detachment, intellectualization, and denial that culture was relevant to understanding psychological development and processes (Atkinson, Morten, & Sue, 1998; Carter, 2005; D. W. Sue & Sue, 2003). Rarely were psychologists challenged to first understand themselves, as recommended by Guideline 1 of the "Guidelines on Multicultural Education, Training, Research, Practice, and Organizational Change for Psychologists" (American Psychological Association [APA], 2003; see also APA Web site version at http://www.apa.org/pi/multiculturalguidelines/). Furthermore, the need to understand the worldviews of ethnoracial minorities has only recently become an area of education and training. More often, stereotypes or broad-brush categorizations were the sources of information for classroom instruction, diagnosis and treatment planning, research hypotheses, and other determinations about what might be good or beneficial for persons of color.

Conclusions about the "Other" have been drawn on the basis of a last name, an accent, phenotype, research specialty, or other indicator of difference from the majority White group. This reductionistic approach also fails to recognize the multiplicity of identities (e.g., dimensions of personal identity), life experiences, and interests held by every individual. Rather than seeing the ethnoracial minority person wholistically, the focus became the visible ethnoracial difference. Janet Helms (1990) spoke of visible ethnic racial groups and automatic negative attributions of lower socioeconomic status, disadvantage, and lower class (Helms & Cook, 1999).

In the cross-cultural communication literature, the term *microaggression* has been used to refer to behaviors, both verbal and nonverbal, that affect the receiver of a message; although the conscious intention may not be to hurt the other, the impact may still be felt. Microaggressions are often uttered in public, professional settings with what the speaker might describe as a "perfectly innocent" question or comment. For example, how often is it assumed that persons of color have been admitted to the university or hired for professional employment because of affirmative action policies? Why is it that persons of color are often expected and asked to represent issues of "their people," then told they are different? Different from whom? Different in what ways? The "lived" examples in Exhibit 3.1 underscore the ways that interpersonal, cross-cultural microaggressions may occur.

EXHIBIT 3.1

Voices Heard

From a Latina professional: "I was the only woman of color in a meeting with a professional women's caucus. At one point, the facilitator noted a concern that there were no women of color in attendance. When I indicated that I was present and Mexican American, the facilitator superficially apologized and said she did not think of me as a minority woman. After all, I was involved in mainstream professional activities."

From an Asian male graduate student: "I have often been told that I am advantaged as an Asian because I am naturally good in math and science and this will help me with psychological research."

From a Latino graduate student: "I have noticed that within graduate student groups, the students of color are the ones primarily interested in the APA Guidelines on Multicultural Education. When we introduce diversity and multicultural focused topics for conference presentations, the White students do not display an interest."

From an African American professional: "Resistance to discussions of diversity is ongoing, consciously or unconsciously. I am continuously bringing up the topic of representation of pluralistic concerns because my colleagues who consider themselves culturally aware do not. Then people say, 'We know we can count on you to keep us honest about diversity issues.'"

From an American Indian researcher: "I get tired of hearing that the money I will pay research participants will likely be spent on alcohol."

Effects of Microaggressions

"Power is often unspoken but a central dynamic in cross-cultural encounters" (Pinderhughes, 1992, p. 109). Pinderhughes further states that these power dynamics communicate attitudes of "dominance, superiority, and denigration . . . better than or less than" (p. 109). The previous examples embody the power dynamics and embedded sentiments of disrespect, hostility, and racism toward the person of color. If the recipient of the microaggression questions or makes a clarification about the statement, she or he is often dismissed further with responses such as "You are too sensitive," "Oh yeah, you know what I mean," or "Sorry, I guess you have to keep us honest." Nonverbal responses also occur when someone is questioned about a dismissive statement. Gestures include rolling of the eyes ("here we go again"), turning away from the speaker, leaving the room when the discussion ensues, or other gestures of disinterest. By applying a perspective-taking or role-taking approach, one can appreciate how emotions would be stirred when disrespect, dismissal, and sentiments of insincerity occur. For most persons of color, microaggressions occur on a daily basis and there is an emotional cumulative effect: being on "attentional overload" (Fiske, 1993, p. 622), feeling the need to overachieve, or even disqualifying pain (Pinderhughes, 1992, p. 124). Fiske (1993) described "attentional overload" as being similar to "hypervigilence," whereby the outsider or minority person must constantly attend to others' interactions with and toward himself or herself. One example is that of an African American male graduate student who was told by his advisor that he needed to get help with his writing, because a previous advisee of this professor, also African American, had poor writing skills. Although the student had been a journalism major, he felt very burdened by this statement and began to obsess about all of his papers. Imagine what it might be like to constantly worry about your writing when you know you have never had problems before.

Another perspective-taking example is provided by McIntosh's (1989) description of the privilege of Whites to be in the company of people who are like them (racially). In chapter 2, examples of self-categorization and self-segregation by ethnoracial minorities were provided as examples of validation and acceptance by their peers. McIntosh's point should not be lost, but quite often it is, for instance, by White people who critically question why people of color tend to "hang together," seemingly oblivious to majority–minority group dynamics.

Microaggressions are often perpetuated by well-meaning individuals who hold egalitarian beliefs but have not (a) processed their negative attitudes and stereotypes about ethnoracial minority groups and (b) had sufficient contact with ethnoracial minority individuals and groups (Ridley, 1995). However, the emotional burden still remains with the Other when intergroup, interpersonal bias occurs.

Contributing Factors to Ethnocentric Worldviews

There is no one explanation for the development of ethnocentric worldviews, because we are all products of individual and group socialization processes. However, the work of anthropologists Kluckhohn and Strodbeck (1961) and E. T. Hall (1976) provides useful reference points for understanding the initial formation of ethnocentric or culture-specific worldviews. A brief discussion of their models and concepts is discussed because these are embedded throughout the Guidelines and are foundational precepts to the way humans think, feel, and act.

WORLDVIEWS

Kluckhohn and Strodbeck (1961) examined groups in their natural cultural settings and on the basis of this research produced a matrix of cultural influences on life issues (see Harris & Moran, 1987). These cultural approaches are framed in question form:

> What is the character of human nature? What is the relationship of man to nature? What is the temporal focus of life? What is the modality of man's activities? And what is the relationship of man/woman to man/woman? (Harris & Moran, 1987, p. 251)

Kluckhohn and Strodbeck found that there are at least three worldviews for each question and that the worldview is influenced by the group's value system. That is, one's primary group of affiliation communicates in word and deed about what is and is not desirable, acceptable, and valued. The three worldviews for "What is the character of human nature?" are "Man is evil, Man is a mixture of good and evil, and Man is good" (Harris & Moran, 1987, p. 251). How we as psychologists characterize human nature derives from what we were taught as children by our family of origin about who to associate with or not, what people were good or evil, and why we were better than another group—usually another ethnic group.

A vivid example of ethnocentric thinking is that of the television character Archie Bunker. Archie had disparaging beliefs about all other ethnic groups, including his Polish son-in-law. One might wonder how his ethnocentrism was formed. Although the program was not deliberately instructive in this regard, it is possible to infer that Archie's early formation in a working class ethnic neighborhood in Chicago with others who were more like him was a primary influence. The second part of this example is that worldviews can change. Although Archie initially judged people from other ethnicities as "evil" or inferior, he moderated this belief once he got to know the individual, they did something for him, or they otherwise demonstrated that they were not like his perception of all of the other group members (Swim & Stangor, 1998).

Subtle or overt reinforced messages become imprinted and part of one's belief system unless there are intervening events or data to change one's worldview. Ibrahim (1984) indicates that a major, life-altering event is generally what may move an individual to another worldview dimension. For example, an individual who views all Middle Eastern persons as evil and likely extremists may moderate his or her view if a Middle Eastern person saves his or her life. Life experiences and contact with those who are "different" are additional influences on a shift in worldview.

Another manifestation of ethnocentric worldviews is through communication patterns. Multicultural psychologists assert that language is a cultural variable and that communication is culture bound. We psychologists, as cultural beings, also have been influenced in our communication practices by our family and other reference groups, including other psychologists. An example comes from the work of E. T. Hall (1976), as discussed in the next subsection.

High Context and Low Context

The concept of "high context" and "low context" was introduced by E. T. Hall in his classic book, *Beyond Culture* (1976). High-context cultures rely more on the unspoken, they are more contextual, and they are what Ramirez and Castañeda (1974) termed "field dependent." Communication is grounded in the context and the person's knowledge of the rules for communicating in this context. Therefore, explicitness of the message is less important than it is in other types of cultures because nonverbal behavior and the context are understood. Communication skills that are taught in U.S. clinical and counselor training programs may work with clients who were socialized with similar forms of messaging, including nonverbal forms, but they may not necessarily be effective in another cultural context.

Cultural groups from the Middle East, Asia, and Latin America are considered to be high context. The United States is categorized as a low-context culture because of the reliance and importance placed on the spoken message. For example, if a Chinese student nods when her professor speaks, this may not mean she is agreeing with what is being said. The nod is an acknowledgment to a person she respects. Professors who grade on class participation often find themselves in a dilemma because they have students who do not speak up because of learned cultural behavior. The issue of low- and high-context culture manifests in teaching, research, clinical practice, and workplace settings. Therefore, we psychologists need to be attuned to this phenomenon so we can respond and model appropriate and flexible behavior for others.

Because cross-cultural communication is essential to the work of psychologists, we discuss one more example from the work of E. T. Hall (1976). Hall used a "cultural iceberg" metaphor to discuss how communication may not always be what one perceives it to be: The formal, or rule-bound, communication behavior is usually above water, and it is these rules that are applied to others. If individuals violate the known, "above-water," rules, they are labeled as "rude," "uncultured," and so forth because they "know better." Continuing with Hall's metaphor, the informal rules are the bottom part of the iceberg. Informal rules are more readily violated because they are not shared by all cultural groups. For instance, for clinicians working with Latino families in psychotherapy, knowing and applying the formal rules of communication are essential in order to prevent microaggressions. A clinician who speaks to the children before the parents, who addresses the parents by their first name instead of "Mr. *X*" and "Mrs. *X*," and who fails to acknowledge the man first would be in clear violation of cultural norms. It is important to know the family rules as well. In some cultures, cross-gender hand-shaking is a cultural violation.

Manifestations of Ethnocentric Thinking

The dimensions of personal identity (DPI; Arredondo & Glauner, 1992) model discussed in chapter 2 suggests that intergroup and intragroup experiences, perceptions, and biases are also formulated on the basis of historical, political, economic, and sociocultural forces. Cultural values, beliefs, norms, and standard acceptable behavior are reinforced by the dominant or prevailing cultural system where one grows up and resides. In the mid-1990s, low-income women were introduced to workforce development opportunities through federal programs. The assumption by those who crafted the legislation (not the women who participated in the program) was that women would experience enhanced self-image, self-esteem, and a sense of personal empowerment. Laudatory reports about the program were often aired on television, with the participants exclaiming how good they felt about themselves in their new clothes and with their newly acquired skills. The dominant assumption that low-income women could be trained was accurate but the follow-through or reinforcement of the skill development did not occur. When the women were ready to enter paid employment, they were faced with an unexpected barrier—the cost of child care.

Several observations of the outcome for the women can be conjectured. On one hand, the policy makers could say that empowerment leads to self-reliance, an individualistic worldview, and therefore the women would need to find a way to cover child care. A collaborative worldview would suggest that the women might continue to require external assistance (reinforcement) until such time as they could pay for all of their living expenses, including child care. Failure to consider the historic and economic context of the Other in this and similar examples may lead to failure of the Other and exasperation by the power brokers, who may believe that people really do not want to be helped or are too lazy to take care of themselves.

INTERACTIVE APPROACHES AND INTERGROUP BIAS

Worldviews begin with primary beliefs and values from one's cultural socialization, reinforced by national or geographic norms (Hofstede, 1980; Kluckhohn & Strodbeck, 1961). This worldview influences attributed value about others who are not like us. Perhaps the best example comes from conceptualization of the hierarchy of the races (Gould, 1994). This theory about the superiority of Caucasians was based on two premises: Caucasians were the most industrious and the most beautiful people the author knew. The fact that he too was Caucasian and that his assertion, without any scientific evidence, became truth is evidence about the power of one's cultural beliefs and values.

Intergroup categorization bias begins with cognitive processes. Similarity and dissimilarity, and the potential benefit from alliances with certain groups of Others, can be calculated on the basis of modeling. Within the practice of psychotherapy, stereotypes about the underutilization of persons of color has led to conclusions at times that this is a form of resistance and apathy. Others have called this behavior "learned helplessness" (Smith, 1985; Spencer, Kim, & Marshall, 1987; Thomas, 1986; Uomoto, 1986). Alternatively, ethnoracial minority college students may be perceived as the ideal candidates for psychotherapy because they are motivated to seek higher education. Although the conditions for the two examples are very disparate, categorization based simply on ethnoracial minority group affiliation, educational background, and perceived motivation leads to different and not always accurate assumptions.

Modeling is another behavior that contributes to "learned" intergroup bias. Female faculty often report that in meetings with peers and students, they experience differential treatment. Students address them by their first name but address their male counterparts as "Dr." Another example comes from an African American professional in a conference setting. She reported to us that after the presentation with men, both ethnoracial minority and White, the students approached the men only, ignoring her completely. According to Exhibit 3.1, intergroup biases are learned. For this example about the conference, it could be hypothesized that sex role stereotyping has contributed to more favorable assumptions about male professors, perhaps causing students not to feel confident and reliant on female professors. Consequentially, students would tend to avoid female professors because they do not value them as they do the men.

Cross-Cultural Communication Norms

Interpersonal interactions introduce a myriad of verbal and nonverbal communication behavior, shaped by gender, race, nationality, age, and other dimensions of personal identity. Communication patterns, styles, symbols, and gestures are highly culture bound and unconsciously scripted. The study of proxemics has informed researchers about nonverbal communication patterns that relate to respectfulness and group identity. Among Latin American, Middle Eastern, and Italian heritage individuals, kissing on the cheek or both cheeks when saying hello is an everyday practice. Furthermore, for many of these same groups, communication patterns vary; social space for persons from the Middle East is considered intimate space by most Americans. Certain behaviors like a Japanese man bowing or a Mauri greeting persons face-to-face to breathe in their breath are all elements of proximity. Another example may relate to creating a learning environment to promote participation. The chairs in a Native American classroom may be in a circle, a sign of collectivism, whereas an American school typically has all chairs facing the teacher.

Furthermore, direct and indirect styles of communication correspond to the concept of high- and low-context cultures. The United States is considered a low-context culture because of the linear and direct style, stereotypically more illustrative of male communication behavior. China, Mexico, and Egypt are termed "high-context cultures" because communication is more contextual, process-oriented, and less rushed.

VERBAL AND NONVERBAL BEHAVIOR

For psychologists, sensitivity and understanding about different cultural scripts for verbal and nonverbal behavior are essential because of differing formal and informal norms across cultures. The United States is considered a very informal culture in contrast to other cultures that are historically older and more formal with respect to communication. For first- and even second-generation college students, calling professors by their first name can engender a sense of shame because they feel they are being disrespectful. The older the individual from most non-U.S. cultures, the more deference and special consideration is expected. For instance, if the therapist is younger than his or her client, then for some, addressing the therapist by his or her first name is considered disrespectful. There must be other considerations of age and gender differences with respect to psychotherapy engagements. In certain cultures, female–male interactions are taboo, from handshaking to individual counseling. These examples suggest that culture-specific knowledge will become necessary in more situations, from the classroom to the therapy office, if we psychologists are to practice ethically (see Exhibit 3.2).

CULTURAL SCRIPTS AND EMOTIONS

Wierzbicka (1994) argued that different cultural attitudes toward emotions influence the "lexicon and grammar of the languages associated with these cultures" (p. 133). She reminds her readers that not all lan-

---

EXHIBIT 3.2

Self-Assessment

Assess your nonverbal and verbal tendencies, as listed next, on a scale of 1–4 (1 = *minimal*; 4 = *always*).

---

minimal (1)   always (4)

- Smile when you agree with what has been said.
- Shake hands with a man but not a woman in a business setting.
- Talk louder when you are working with a person with an accent that makes you uncomfortable.
- Stop listening when a peer begins to talk about multicultural issues.
- Interrupt a younger colleague at a faculty meeting.

---

guages have lexicons to accommodate the emotional terms that are most familiar in English such as *sad, happy, disgusted, sorry, delighted,* and so forth. When these emotions are discussed in other languages, much more of the subjective experience is often shared, involving many more words and different meanings, because there is not always a simple translation from English. For example, for Chinese speakers, the term *shame* is an emotion held by the individual for himself or herself, whereas *guilt* is more collectivistic, also encompassing feelings for self and one's family.

In Spanish, the use of reflexive pronouns conveys "ownership" for the emotion. An exchange between two Spanish speakers, a therapist and a patient, might be as follows (an asterisk after a word indicates it is a reflexive pronoun):

> *Therapist:* Juanita, cómo te* encuentras hoy? [Literal translation: "Juanita, how are you finding yourself today?" Translation: "Juanita, how do you feel today?"]
>
> *Juanita:* Bueno, Dra. Fouad, me* siento muy mal; no sé si me* explico bien. [Translation: "Well, Dr. Fouad, I am feeling myself very poorly; I don't know whether I am making myself understood."]

Unconscious Dynamics and Their Effects

Well-meaning individuals can still do harm, because they may have too many unexamined assumptions about ethnoracial minorities. In the previous chapter, we discussed the minority identity development model (Atkinson et al., 1998) and suggested that ethnoracial minorities may also operate from unconscious biases. The net effect of unexamined intergroup biases may be aversive racism (Gaertner & Dovidio, 2000).

Aversive Racism

Aversive racism is presumed to be characteristic of well-educated and liberal Whites and other groups that support and promote egalitarianism and social sensitivity (Gaertner & Dovidio, 2000). This explanation lends support to Guideline 2, which emphasizes "the importance of multicultural sensitivity/responsiveness, knowledge of, and understanding about ethnically and racially different individuals" (APA, 2003, p. 385). Interpersonally, ethnoracial minorities can recognize the feelings of mistrust of aversive racists. The feeling of knowing who is an explicit and expressive racist is helpful to ethnoracial minorities so that these individuals (the racist) can be readily identified, their behavior processed according to their value system, and the interaction filtered rather than immediately personalized. On the other hand, aversive racism makes ethnoracial minorities feel insecure because of the unknown or hidden agendas that lie below the surface in interactions. This insecurity can manifest itself in defensive ways such as assimilating to the dominant culture to avoid dealing with intergroup differences, withdrawing into an ethnocentric posture to insulate feelings of cultural pride and to minimize or suppress thoughts of difference, becoming hypersensitive to comments and issues of cultural identity in an attempt to ward off offensive comments, and becoming numb and accustomed to racist inferences as they occur. Aversive racists feel ambivalent toward people of color engendering tensions but the burden of dealing with these tensions lies with the Other, in these examples, ethnoracial minorities.

"The ambivalence associated with aversive racism is rooted in the conflict between feelings and values" (Gaertner & Dovidio, 2000, p. 13) toward the Other although this is also situational. How one may feel toward an undocumented immigrant Latino male who stands in a parking lot on a daily basis, hoping someone will offer him employment for the day will likely vary toward another undocumented immigrant who is asking for a handout. One may feel ambivalent toward both because of their undocumented status but less critical of the man who is seeking to work.

Aversive racists may have genuinely good intentions with social justice platforms and may be champions of indigent and marginalized causes; however, they also have discomfort with ethnoracial minority power. The challenge of aversive racism exists for both White and ethnoracial minority psychologists. As Gaertner and Dovidio (2000) stated, "This type of subtle, unintentional bias that is reflected in aversive racism is particularly resistant to change" (p. 14), differing from explicit racial prejudice that has declined over time.

Negative Effects of Social Control

Well-meaning individuals would not like to believe that they can control anyone other than themselves. Beliefs about autonomy and self-sufficiency are consistent with the U.S. worldview of individualism. However, historically, social control has been enacted toward ethnoracial minorities and members of other marginalized groups (e.g., disabled, poor). Those who have power tend to engage in stereotyping behavior, giving them the upper hand and control (Fiske, 1993) in interpersonal relationships. Social control is a dynamic that affects the Other, and there appears to be a direct link to aversive racism. Fiske (1993) has stated, "Stereotyping operates in the service of control" (p. 623). Although we are both professional women, stereotypes held about ethnoracial minorities may be a form of social control attributed to us. We can stay within the limits of a stereotype and, for example, be the mother of three children, or we can contradict the stereotype by being a married Latina without children. Not conforming to the expectant stereotypical behavior can "disappoint the holder of the stereotype" (Fiske, 1993, p. 623; see Exhibit 3.3).

For us as psychologists, the potential for social control is constant because we are not immune to stereotypes we have learned and that are reinforced on a daily basis. Thus, it is essential to be mindful of situations in which forms of social control may be inadvertently applied. In the previous chapter, several examples were offered about attributions based on singular and multiple dimensions of personal identity. Additional examples are expecting White male students to do well with statistics but not African American male students, assuming that ethnoracial minority researchers are only interested in working on ethnic issues and with ethnic minority students, sending all Asian clients to the Chinese American psychologist in the counseling center, and discouraging students from examining racial–cultural variables in research because they are too complex. As faculty, clinical staff, and researchers, we may not see the overview of power and social control, but it affects cross-cultural relationships.

Invisibility Syndrome

There are multiple contradictions for persons of color in social contact on a day-to-day basis in racially stratified U.S. society. On the one hand,

EXHIBIT 3.3

Social Control

■ With whom do you assert social control? Are these individuals more culturally similar or dissimilar to you?

■ If you are not African American and you have an African American client who indicates she prefers to work with you rather than an African American therapist, are you confused? How might social control explain her behavior?

■ When you are teaching a class on personality, do you tell students that cross-cultural issues are not relevant?

■ Do you tell your research class that science is color blind?

Helms (1984) indicated that being seen as a visible ethnic racial group results in attributions and misattributions that adversely affect in-group–out-group relations. On the other hand, despite persons of color continuing to aspire to move up the career ladder, to improve the quality of their lives and their families' lives, and to live with dignity and respect, acknowledgment of these efforts has not been forthcoming, as demonstrated by economics.

In a very powerful book on Black men and their dreams, Franklin (2004) introduced the concept of the "invisibility syndrome." Drawing on narratives from men he met with in clinical practice, he repeatedly heard stories of frustrated dreams, daily indignities, lost promotions and plum job assignments, and being ignored when ideas were shared. Not being noticed by the cab driver or the store clerk, not having a workplace mentor, and being left out of the important business decisions are examples of the invisibility syndrome.

Intergroup Contact

In multicultural psychology, participation versus observation, field experiences instead of only textbook knowledge, and immersion into a different cultural experience are recommended to heighten awareness about the Other, as of course is engaging in live intergroup contact. Relevant to this discussion is the concept of "boundaries" and the role that psychological boundaries play in the formation, maintenance, and transformation of identities—self and other. All people have emotional bases of identity that affect interpersonal relationships. "'Identity-defining boundaries' are considerably influenced by negative feelings" (Benson, 2003, p. 61). How people perceive themselves will influence whom they choose to speak with (action boundary) and whom they stay away from (body boundary). These are part of psychological boundaries at the onset or in consideration of intergroup contact.

SIMILARITY

Perceived similarity is another positive enabler to inter- and intragroup contact or integration. Clothing, religious symbols, and colors are examples of possible similarity at a more visible level. Many adolescent cocultures place an importance on style because it is how they can identify in-group and out-group members (e.g., different sororities wear different colors and lettering to identify allegiance). The appearance of Hasidic Jews, Muslim women, and American Indian elders signals similarity and reduces psychological boundaries for some individuals.

To the outsider, similarity and perceived similarity may be at odds. The culturally uninformed researcher may want to have American Indians in a research study but fail to be sensitive to tribal differences. As another example, in the late 1980s, there were refugees from El Salvador and Nicaragua who had different political affiliations. It would have been a mistake to assume that a shared national heritage made these individuals similar in all regards. Quite often, the political animosities continued in the United States.

The DPI can be incorporated into this discussion. There is a greater tendency to assume similarities based on the more visible A Dimensions (e.g., age, gender), when in fact the less visible B Dimensions (education, pastimes) may be the more critical point of connection. Among professionals, it is far easier to discuss one's research with others who share a similar agenda. Specialty areas breed similarities. However, this may not occur uniformly among professionals. Thus, we psychologists need to be mindful of identity-defining boundaries, aversive racism, and stereotyping that may prevent engagement with the Other.

CONTACT HYPOTHESIS

For psychologists, education and employment place us in contact with others of different backgrounds and heritage, including ethnoracial minorities. The contact hypothesis suggests that intergroup cooperation "reduces the salience of the intergroup boundary" (Gaertner & Dovidio, 2000, p. 73) while it reduces bias. When there is cooperative interdependence (teamwork), personalization, and equity in status, positive intergroup attitudes may develop. There are many examples through involvement with APA that demonstrate this concept. The criteria for board and committee elections often outline specific and general qualifications bringing psychologists who would otherwise not work together, engaged for a

EXHIBIT 3.4

Interpersonal Contact

▪ How often do you have contact with individuals with differing dimensions of personal identity?

▪ What is your comfort level when there is forced contact with ethnoracial minorities on a committee or task force at work or within APA?

▪ Diversity is described as an enabler of cultural enrichment. Would you agree or disagree? Why or why not?

professional agenda. Biases based on specialties, science versus practice orientations, and other within-association difference become minimized because of the mandate to work toward a common goal. For some ethnoracial minority and White psychologists, APA may be a setting for initial contact; see Exhibit 3.4 for an activity relating to these initial-contact situations.

Summary

Multicultural psychology has been clear in its attention to context, interpersonal connections for individuals and groups, and the conundrum of universality and relativity. For some, the latter is also indicative of culture-specific behavior (D. W. Sue & Sue, 2003). The development of understanding from multiple perspectives is another criterion from the Guidelines, inviting psychologists to engage in flexible thinking and adaptive behaviors. From the cognitive emerges the affective or emotional aspect of multicultural competency that begins with multicultural awareness and sensitivity. For psychologists who are researchers, academics, clinicians, or administrators, alignment of our cognitions and emotions will serve to accurately engage in culturally responsive behaviors.

In this chapter, we psychologists have been encouraged to heed Guideline 2 and "to recognize the importance of multicultural sensitivity/responsiveness to, knowledge of, and understanding about ethnically and racially different individuals" (APA, 2003, p. 385). To help heighten sensitivity and knowledge, we discussed several interpersonal and intergroup concepts. Readers have been invited to assume responsibility for their cross-cultural self-assessment and ongoing cultural competency development. Although Guideline 2 suggests learning more culture-specific information, the space constraints of this chapter prevented us from exploring that in detail.

In this chapter, we also reviewed the importance of the power dynamics of aversive racism, identity boundaries, microaggressions, and social control. Because we are all cultural beings, we have learned and have had the privilege of applying these power dynamics with the Other, often the ethnoracial minority woman or man. To decrease intergroup stigmatization, hostility, and clashes, we should all be mindful about unconscious emotions based on racial–cultural differences.

Finally, we psychologists have the responsibility and opportunity to develop cultural competency about the Other. When working with a particular population of clients, students, or peers, psychologists are encouraged to become knowledgeable about how history has been different for the major U.S. cultural groups. Second, psychologists should evaluate their comfort level with different ethnoracial minority group members and determine why there is discomfort. Third, we should realize that ethnoracial minority individuals hold multiple identities, and we should consider the whole person. Fourth, we should keep in mind that cultural competency personal development is a lifelong process.

Implications for Psychologists as Practitioners

4

What we think, or what we know, or what we believe is, in the end, of little consequence. The only consequence is what we do.

—John Ruskin

Guideline 5: Psychologists are encouraged to apply culturally appropriate skills in clinical and other applied psychological practices.[1]

Competency Statements

Psychologists who use the constructs of "multiculturalism" and "diversity" in psychological practice will be able to

- understand the need for culture-centered psychological practice in effective treatment of all clients;
- recognize that discrimination and oppression (e.g., ethnocentrism, racism, sexism, ableism, homophobia) may relate to presenting psychological concerns;
- recognize potential reasons that clients of color are underrepresented in those seeking and staying in treatment;
- recognize culturally relevant factors that may be included in a client's history; and
- understand the need to develop a repertoire of treatments specific to a client's culture.

Overview

Culture-centered psychological practice was the first area of concern for multicultural scholars. In 1982, a Division 17 (Society of Counseling Psy-

---

[1]Cited in "Guidelines on Multicultural Education, Training, Research, Practice, and Organizational Change for Psychologists," American Psychological Association (APA; 2003, p. 390; see also APA Web site version at http://www.apa.org/pi/multiculturalguidelines/).

chology) task force report (D. W. Sue et al., 1982) charged that traditional counseling practices were "demanding, irrelevant, and oppressive
toward the culturally different" (p. 45) and set out the need for psychologists to develop cultural competence in awareness, knowledge, and
skills. Twenty years later, their charge was echoed by the U.S. Surgeon
General's report, *Mental Health: Culture, Race, and Ethnicity* (U.S. Department of Health and Human Services [USDHHS], 2001); the task force
concluded, "Racial and ethnic minorities have less access to mental health
services than do Whites. They are less likely to receive needed care. When
they receive care, it is more likely to be poor in quality" (p. 3). The U.S.
Surgeon General's report noted that barriers stem from a variety of reasons, which include the stigma associated with seeking mental health
help but also "clinicians' lack of awareness of cultural issues, bias, or
inability to speak the client's language, and the client's fear and mistrust
of treatment" (p. 3).

This chapter focuses on the development of culturally appropriate
psychological applications. We build on the information in chapters 2
and 3 and assume that we psychologists have an awareness and knowledge about our own worldview as cultural beings and as professional
psychologists and have an understanding of the worldview of others,
particularly as influenced by ethnic/racial heritage, before applying this
understanding to our practice with clients. We define *psychological practice*
as the use of psychological skills in a variety of settings and for a variety
of purposes, encompassing counseling, clinical, school, consulting, and
organizational psychology. We argue in this chapter that psychologists
are most effective when they are able to incorporate culture-centered
adaptations in interventions and practices. This is consistent with Principle E (Respect for People's Rights and Dignity) of the American Psychological Association's (APA's) "Ethical Principles of Psychologists and Code
of Conduct" (APA, 2002; see also APA Web site version at http://
www.apa.org/ethics/), which states,

> Psychologists are aware of and respect cultural, individual, and role
> differences, including those based on age, gender, gender identity, race,
> ethnicity, culture, national origin, religion, sexual orientation,
> disability, language, and socioeconomic status and consider these
> factors when working with members of such groups. Psychologists try
> to eliminate the effect on their work of biases based on those factors,
> and they do not knowingly participate in or condone activities of
> others based upon such prejudices. (p. 1063)

As we noted in chapter 1, we psychologists are increasingly likely to
find ourselves working with clients who are different from us, which
may include different in ethnicity, language, and race. It is critical to note
that clients may differ on several dimensions that may or may not be
immediately visible to the counselor or therapist (Carter, 1995; Helms,

1995; Herring, 1999; Hong & Ham, 2001; Niemann, 2001; Padilla, 1995; Santiago-Rivera, Arredondo, & Gallardo-Cooper, 2002; D. W. Sue & Sue, 1999; Vandiver, 2001). A major challenge for culture-centered psychologists is that these dimensions can easily include the client's language, gender, biracial or multiracial heritage, spiritual and religious orientations, sexual orientation, age, disability, socioeconomic situation, and historical life experience (e.g., immigration and refugee status), and any of these dimensions can interact with each other (Arredondo, 2002; Constantine, 2002; Harley, Jolivette, McCormick, & Tice, 2002; Hong & Ham, 2001; Lowe & Mascher, 2001; Prendes-Lintel, 2001). Some of these dimensions may be more salient at one time than at another, and an effective therapist is aware of how cultural dimensions may affect a client but also remains flexible enough to understand when those dimensions conflict or are less salient to the particular issue the client brings to the therapy. Consider Case Vignette 1, later in this section, about Carmen. The counseling center psychologist conducted a very typical intake session for a college student who may be depressed, assessing depth of depression and risk of suicide. Clearly, such an assessment is wholly appropriate and necessary because Carmen may, indeed, be at risk for depression and may benefit from medication. But the therapist did not understand the additional stressors that Carmen faced as a Mexican American daughter away from home, where her family's tradition valued the role of the daughter at home as a support to her mother, and the stressors that she faced because her boyfriend expected her to have a traditional role. The psychologist did not understand that Carmen might be conflicted between two cultures, her Mexican American roots and the European American college environment, and that she might feel embarrassed at disclosing such a conflict.

Carmen's decision to not go back for further counseling highlights the findings from the Surgeon General's report (USDHHS, 2001). Although the United States is more culturally diverse than ever in its history, individuals seeking and staying in psychological treatment continue to primarily be European American. Some reasons that ethnoracial minorities are underrepresented in psychological services include the lack of cultural sensitivity of therapists and distrust of services by ethnoracial clients (D. W. Sue & Sue, 1999), although the U.S. Surgeon General's report documents that ethnoracial minority clients need psychological services. D. W. Sue and Sue (2003) noted that often "mental health professionals are surprised to find that there is a high incidence of psychological distress in the minority community, that their treatment techniques do not work, and that the culturally different do not use their services" (p. 44).

D. W. Sue and Sue (2003) pointed out that the values on which most traditional, Eurocentric therapeutic and interventions models are based are quite different from the values embraced by many ethnoracial minority clients. They delineate values of class, culture, and language that are often endorsed unconsciously by therapists, leveling the charge that therapists are so embedded in these values that they do not realize they impose those values on others. Class-bound values include a rigid emphasis on a time schedule, unstructured approach, and insight orientation with a focus on long-term goals. D. W. Sue and Sue noted that poverty and ethnoracial minority status are intertwined, and many middle-class therapists are unaware of situations in which a client does not own a car, relies on public transportation, and is less able to meet strict time schedules. Also, they noted that therapy focused on gaining insight is unwanted for many minority clients who are seeking tangible solutions to problems that involve basic needs such as shelter and food.

Culture-bound values include an overemphasis on the individual (whereas many ethnoracial minority clients value their families and extended kinship networks) and expectations that clients will be verbally expressive, open, comfortable with verbal intimacy, and appreciate a linear approach to problem solving. Carmen's counselor, for example, placed too much emphasis on her as an independent individual, rather than focusing also on her within the context of her family. Finally, as D. W. Sue and Sue (2003) noted, as the United States is becoming increasingly culturally diverse, it is also becoming increasingly multilingual; they point out that therapists who insist on Standard English or who cannot provide bilingual services may not be meeting the needs of their clients.

We are suggesting that it is important for psychologists to enhance their cultural sensitivity and understanding to be the most effective as practitioners. The checklist in Appendix A outlines the critical components that we feel encompass cultural competence for practitioners. We divide the discussion in this chapter into three areas: focusing on clients within their cultural contexts, using culturally appropriate assessment tools, and developing a broad repertoire of interventions.

Case Vignette 1: Carmen

Carmen, who is Mexican American, seeks help at the University Counseling Center at the advice of her European American roommate, because she is considering dropping out of college, even though she is doing quite well academically. She is struggling with a conflict between wanting to be in college and seeking a career as an accountant, on the one hand, and the lack of support from her parents and her *novio* (boyfriend), on the other. Her mother and father are not supportive of her being so far away from home, her mother cries every time she calls, and Carmen feels guilty that she is not home to help out with her younger siblings. Her boyfriend also does not support her wanting to be in college or seeking a career, because he hopes that she will be home with their children.

When she arrives at the University Counseling Center, she is embarrassed to immediately talk to the psychologist about her family, because they are so different from everyone else's in her dorm, so she does not bring up her family. Her presenting concern to her counselor is that she does not feel that she "fits" at the university, and she talks about her roommate, her classes, and being away from home. The counselor's questions at the first interview center around her sleeping behavior (she is sleeping a lot), her eating (she has lost 15 pounds in the past 2 months), and whether she considers suicide (she does not, because she is Catholic and believes suicide would be a sin). The counselor's diagnosis is that she is depressed but not suicidal, and she refers her to a psychiatrist for antidepressants. Carmen leaves the session vowing not to return, because the therapist never once asked her about her family or the other conflicts in her life.

Case Vignette 2: Vera

Vera came to discuss her marriage and her confusion about being married to a man she does not love and who is not maintaining his commitment to the marriage. Vera was raised in Bombay, India, and is studying for her master's degree in computer science at a major university in Massachusetts. Upon completion of her studies, her parents reminded her of her duty to marry. Vera complied with her parents' request and entered an arranged marriage. Her husband was selected by a non-family member, an individual in the "business" of matchmaking. Now Vera finds herself with a depressed husband without a job. He too has a master's degree in accounting, but he cannot seem to find employment. Consequently, he remains at home, passing the time looking at want ads, and otherwise, withdrawing from Vera. She does not want to complain to her parents, and she wonders about the possibility of leaving her marriage. Vera is in a cultural quandary. Her husband has very little to offer her and she does not love him but she wants to respect her parents' wishes.

Case Vignette 3: Harold

Harold is a senior manager in a global organization, and he considers himself a "humanist." He was charged with the company's diversity initiative. Harold enjoyed spiritual readings and everything having to do with issues of race and culture in the workplace. A college graduate, he has a successful track record in finance for the company for whom he has worked for more than 20 years. Harold was proud of the CEO's invitation to lead the diversity initiative and indicated that he wanted to represent the issues and make the company look good at the same time.

Harold seeks counseling 2 years into the initiative. He indicates that at every turn in his plans, it seems as though he is being thwarted. Suddenly he is being challenged for decisions he had made. His boss tells him that he is spending too much money on the initiative and is making a big deal out of small issues. African American employees are critical also, telling Harold that they expected more from him since he was one of them. He is beginning to doubt his ability to lead and is also feeling that his peers and boss now view him differently. "I think my race is a problem here," he says. "They seem to be scrutinizing every move I make. I'm not having much fun. Maybe I should just take early retirement and leave," he laments.

Client in Context

It is critical that psychologists approach each client with a commitment to understand the client within his or her context(s). Clients' contexts are shaped by multiple levels of experiences. We discussed the personal dimensions of identity in chapter 2. A client's identity is shaped by his or her A Dimensions, which include such factors as culture, gender, race, age, language, and sexual orientation experiences, as well as his or her C Dimensions, which are determined by the way that the A Dimension identity has been treated historically. It is the B Dimensions (a combination of A and C Dimensions) that often shape the context for clients. Clients' health and mental health experiences, their experiences with discrimination and oppression (e.g., ethnocentrism, racism, sexism, ableism, and homophobia), their relationship status, and their opportunities for work and education all shape the context in which they live. Thus, it is critical that psychologists understand how these various experiences affect the concerns that clients bring to treatment (Byars & McCubbin, 2001; Flores & Carey, 2000; Helms & Cook, 1999; Herring, 1999; Hong & Ham, 2001; Lowe & Mascher, 2001; D. W. Sue & Sue, 2003).

A variety of additional factors may affect the context of the client, as well. For example, for many clients, generational history may be important. Questions may include how many generations of their family have been in the United States and how the family entered the country. The context for African American clients whose families came to this country as slaves may be quite different from those who came to this country from Africa to seek higher education. For others, fleeing a violent regime in their country of origin may carry with it a trauma not present in those who sought to immigrate in more peaceful times. Similarly, questions may include status of citizenship or residence, including parental history of immigration and number of years in the country. Contextual factors for those who are first generation (born in the United States) are quite different for those who are recent immigrants, and yet again quite different from those who have been in the United States a number of generations. The first generation are often the most interested in assimilating into the mainstream culture, frequently setting up a conflict with their immigrant parents who may want to retain traditional cultural behavior. This is exacerbated when there is a demotion in social status as a result of coming to this country, when, for example, professional degrees or family ties are not recognized in the United States. Additional factors that affect clients' context include number of languages spoken (and comfort with English), the level of family support and functionality, availability of community resources, level of education, work history, and level of stress related to acculturation (Arredondo, 2002; Root, 1999; Ruiz, 1990; Saldana, 1995; Smart & Smart, 1995).

Consider the context for Carmen in Case Vignette 1. Her context is shaped by being a woman of Mexican American heritage. We do not know how long her family has been in the United States but it does appear that they hold traditional values with regard to the role of women in the family. Carmen seems to have a strong relationship with her family and her boyfriend. Her current living context is in a primarily White university dorm, which is a distance from her family. She appears to be at a stage of ethnic identity in which she is conflicted about seeming "different" from others, yet she is pulled by the traditional values of her family. She may be assumed to be bright, because she is doing well academically. Carmen's counselor did not approach her from the perspective of her cultural background and thus missed an opportunity to be of help to her. We would have recommended that the counselor ask Carmen how she is feeling about being so far from home and how her family is feeling. The counselor could also have asked Carmen how she decided to go to that specific university and could have helped her to clarify how she feels about that decision now. The counselor could have also followed up with helping Carmen to clarify the conflict she feels between pursuing an individual goal versus a goal valued by her family (returning home).

The second vignette, about Vera, also points out the importance of understanding the client in his or her context—in this case, Vera's context is as a woman of Indian nationality here in the United States to study. She follows the cultural norms of entering into an arranged marriage at the request of her parents. It may be tempting for a U.S. therapist to treat this as a fairly straightforward situation of a woman trapped in a loveless marriage and help her to get a divorce. The therapist's beliefs about marriage may enter into this view as well, particularly if the therapist values marriage as a love relationship between two individuals. But Vera's cultural context has a different view of marriage as between two families rather than two individuals, and she may have a strong commitment to respect the marriage arranged by her parents. Expectations of love, as defined in the United States, may not enter into her decision making. However, Vera has lived in the United States for several years, and her immersion in U.S. culture is part of her context. Her therapist could help her to explore how she feels about her marriage, what her expectations are about marriage, and what might be the cultural consequences of ending it. By *cultural consequences*, we mean the consequences that Vera might encounter by taking steps that are out of her culture's norm. For example, will her parents be unhappy with her; will they view this as a mark of disrespect? How will she feel, going against the expectations of marriage and the role of women in keeping a marriage together in her culture?

In Case Vignette 3, Harold's cultural context is shaped by his race, as well as by his experiences in the company and his experiences with discrimination. Harold's experiences with discrimination help to shape his view that the reactions to his work on the diversity initiative are based on reactions to race. His boss, who is White, is critical and appears not to value the work that Harold has done, apparently not supporting him at times when Harold has called attention to concerns (e.g., his boss makes statements about Harold "making a big deal out of small issues"). Harold's African American colleagues feel he hasn't made enough of a big deal out of things. He appears to be caught between wanting to do things to support diversity but is criticized for doing too much or not doing enough. His therapist should talk with him about his perceptions of how his race has affected his supervisor's views of him and whether he feels he is able to do the work to his satisfaction. He doubts his ability to lead, but the therapist may want to help Harold see how much of others' reactions to his leadership are due to his own ability (an internal problem) or to racism (an external problem). His therapist may also want to help Harold explore how he feels about confronting the racism at his work and to help Harold think through ways that he can do that constructively. The therapist may want to think about ways that she or he could help be an advocate for Harold, to help him combat the racism at his company. If Harold does not want to fight the racism there anymore, the therapist may want to help him think through how ready he is for retirement and what the consequences of taking early retirement may be. Questions the therapist may ask include the following: How will this impact your family financially? What activities will you do after you retire (how will you spend your time)? How prepared are you emotionally for this transition? How will you feel if you do not go back and fight the racism there? How might you feel if you do fight the racism and it makes no difference?

As we hope is evident from our discussion of Case Vignettes 1–3, understanding the client in context is not done with one specific strategy or technique. Rather, the therapist brings his or her understanding of possible cultural hypotheses for a client's concerns, and flexibly applies that understanding. Culturally competent practitioners use that flexibility to know that although they have knowledge of a client's cultural background, not everyone in that culture is the same nor does every client incorporate all aspects of that culture. As we note in chapter 6, one of the criticisms of psychological research is the assumption that all individuals of an ethnoracial group are the same. A similar criticism is leveled at psychological practitioners who apply knowledge about cultural norms and values to all members of a group without appreciating the great within-group differences for each group. Differences within ethnoracial groups may be due to a wide variety of factors, including gender, age, social class, educational level, and sexual orientation. It is critical that psychologists not rigidly stereotype all members of a group. As the Council of National Psychological Associations for the Advancement of Ethnic Minority Interests (CNPAAEMI) noted about their recommendations on psychological treatment, "These recommendations should never be applied rigidly without regard for individual differences, subgroup variations, and the specific life circumstance of clients. To do so borders on stereotyping and would prove more harmful than helpful" (2003, p. 3).

One final area of understanding the clients in their cultural contexts is to appreciate the role of racism in the issues that ethnoracial minority clients may bring to therapy. It is important to help clients understand whether their concern or problem stems from institutional or societal racism, sexism, classism, or homophobia rather than from an internal cause. Part of this includes helping clients recognize whether and when they are targets of prejudice and how that may affect their thinking or behavior (Crocker, Major, & Steele, 1998). It also includes understanding the stressors that stem from coping with racism (CNPAAEMI, 2003).

Assessment

We discuss culturally appropriate assessment in chapter 6, focusing on the use of culturally valid instruments in research. It is equally important to use culturally valid instruments in psychological practice. Consistent with Standards 9.02b and 9.06 of the APA Ethics Code, culturally competent practitioners only use assessment instruments whose validity and reliability have been established for use with members of the population tested, and they take the client's personal, linguistic, and cultural differences into account when interpreting assessment results. A number of authors have expressed strong concern about the inappropriate use of assessment tools with ethnoracial minorities, including concerns with misdiagnosing psychopathology (Constantine, 1998; Helms, 2002; Ridley, Hill, & Li, 1998; D. W. Sue & Sue, 2003). Assessment in therapy, broadly defined, encompasses all aspects of gathering information about a client. This may be via written intake forms, initial interviews for data gathering purposes, and traditional assessment tools. Too often, therapists assume that clients are familiar with mental health services and that they are familiar with the process of filling out forms prior to therapy. However, if a client is not familiar with this process, or if the client is offended by a therapist's method of systematically gathering information, this process may seem cold and the client may feel disrespected. We encourage therapists to fully explain procedures; to be sensitive to the needs of the client, which should take precedence over filling out paperwork; and to focus on building a culturally appropriate relationship with a client. Ridley et al. (1998) recommended gathering data from multiple sources, including interviews, life histories, and behavioral observations.

We cannot stress enough how important it is for psychologists to know whether an instrument or procedure is valid for use with the client's population. This includes ascertaining its appropriateness prior to administering it to a client and then interpreting the information from the instrument appropriately. Ridley et al. (1998) called this the "interpreting cultural data" phase. Included in this phase are steps to determine whether the information gathered from the client is cultural or individual, to ascertain the role of environmental stressors on the client's behavior, and to determine what part of the data is clinically significant. If therapists use standardized assessment tools and methods, particularly those that may have high-stakes results (e.g., resulting in an educational or work placement), they also use care and critical judgment in interpreting the results (Sandoval, Frisby, Geisinger, Scheuneman, & Grenier, 1998). Finally, culture-centered psychologists are encouraged to consider what Messick (1995) termed "consequential validity," or the short- and long-term consequences of the instrument used. This includes not only understanding issues related to test bias, test fairness, and cultural equivalence but also anticipating, as much as possible, the consequences of the testing itself. For example, the social and political results of the controversy on intelligence testing, described in chapter 6, may result in consequences for an ethnoracial minority client asked to complete an intelligence test, not only from the results of the test but also from being asked to take such a test. Psychologists need to carefully weigh the potential consequences for clients.

Interventions

We also think it is important for psychologists to learn about helping and healing practices used in non-Western cultures. It is ironic that the traditional Western individual therapy, formed only 100 years ago, has become the standard helping model, when there have been people assigned as healers and helpers in most cultures throughout history. Non-Western or indigenous ways of helping and healing include the Native American sweat lodge, shaman spiritualism, and *curanderos* (spiritual healer from Mexico). D. W. Sue and Sue (2003) pointed out that although specific indigenous healing methods vary widely by culture, there are some commonalities. These include relying on the group or family to help the individual make a collective (rather than individual) decision, incorporating spiritual beliefs into the healing, and the healing being conducted by a wise person or elder with special talents. We encourage psychologists to become familiar with the various forms of healing and to know that effective therapy may require nontraditional interventions. For example, psychologists can reach out to meet recognized helpers in the community and seek their advice on assessment and intervention plans. We suggest that psychologists learn more about the communities in which their clients reside, for instance, reading the local newspaper, and when appropriate, participating in community events.

The final area in culturally competent practice is to develop a repertoire of skills and practices that may be effectively used with the unique worldview and cultural backgrounds of clients. Psychologists can do this by explicitly incorporating an understanding of their client's context, as we discussed earlier, into the interventions and treatments chosen. One way to begin to do this is to become familiar with authors who write from a culture centered perspective. For example, the CNPAAEMI (2003) has published a primer on psychological treatment of ethnic minority populations that includes specific recommendations for treatment of different groups, as do D. W. Sue and Sue (2003) and McGoldrick, Giordano, and Pearce (1996). Other authors write about specific groups, such as Latinos/Hispanics (Falicov, 1999; Flores & Carey, 2000; Santiago-Rivera et al., 2002), Asian Americans (Chien & Banerjee, 2002; Hong & Ham, 2001; Sue, 2001; Tien & Olson, 2003), African Americans (Boyd-Franklin, 2001, 2003; Hall & Greene, 2003), and Native Americans/American Indians (Garrett, Garrett, & Brotherton, 2001; Herring, 1999; LaFromboise

EXHIBIT 4.1

Reviewing Case Vignettes

Consider Case Vignettes 1–3. How might you answer the following questions?

1. What interventions would you use with each case, Carmen, Vera, and Harold?
2. How might your interventions be different if Carmen was African American?
3. How might your interventions be different if Vera was White European American?
4. How might your interventions be different if Harold was American Indian?
5. Are there ways that you might include community helpers in any of the cases? How would you go about involving them?
6. What might be your own personal biases or values that would affect your counseling with each case?

& Dizon, 2003; LaFromboise & Jackson, 1996; LaFromboise, Trimble, Mohatt, 1998; Warner, 2003). In addition, some authors write about the intersections of other dimensions of identity and race/ethnicity, such as spirituality (e.g., Fukuyama & Sevig, 1999; Langman, 1998), sexual orientation (Fukuyama & Ferguson, 2000), and disability (Middleton, Rollins, & Harley, 1999).

It is important that we psychologists understand our power as therapists. This power may be attributed to our advanced educational level, the use of the formal title "Dr.," our social class, and our race. Power is inherent in the role of the therapist, and effective therapists know the impact of our power in helping clients. D. W. Sue and Sue (2003) commented on the social power that counselors have over clients that facilitates change, reviewing the research that shows that trust in the power of the therapist is a critical component in the therapeutic relationship. Consistent with our discussions in chapter 2, central to becoming a culturally competent practitioner is an understanding of our power, and more critically, taking care not to abuse that power. But, understanding the role of power also suggests that psychologists also understand the power relationships within ethnoracial minority families and that we take care not to violate those relationships. For example, the use of children as translators may put children and parents in a very uncomfortable position, violating the power that parents usually have to control information.

Finally, in addition to learning more about culture-specific interventions and non-Western practices, we culturally competent practitioners should examine the cultural appropriateness of our traditional psycho-

EXHIBIT 4.2

When Are Interventions Culturally Appropriate?

Questions for practitioners to ask:

1. Am I conducting therapy in a language that my client is comfortable speaking? Is it my client's native tongue? If not, how might that affect my client's level of anxiety in expressing himself or herself? How may language affect my client's memory of childhood events?
2. How may my client interpret my nonverbal behavior? Do my nonverbal cues match well with my client's? How might I be aware if my client is culturally uncomfortable with my nonverbal behavior?
3. What are my client's expectations of counseling? How might those expectations be culturally determined? How should I modify my therapy to meet my client's goals for therapy?
4. How will I know whether my traditional therapeutic techniques are culturally inappropriate?
5. How might I modify my traditional therapeutic techniques to be more appropriate?
6. How might I incorporate my client's spiritual and religious beliefs if they are powerful sources of support for my client?
7. How important is my client's family to him or her? How can I help my client identify strengths and resources from his or her family and community?
8. Do I need to become an advocate for my client? Are his or her problems or concerns beyond the scope of individual therapy, and is there a role I can play in advocating for institutional or societal change?

therapy interventions. (Consider Case Vignettes 1–3 and the activity in Exhibit 4.1. How might practitioners develop culturally appropriate interventions to work with Carmen, Vera, or Harold? We suggest that practitioners might ask themselves the questions in Exhibit 4.2.) This includes respecting the language preference of the client and understanding that sometimes emotions are best expressed in one's native tongue. Consistent with an awareness of self, we encourage psychologists to understand their own nonverbal behavior and how that might be interpreted by culturally different clients, seeking consultation with others if need be to help answer that question. We encourage psychologists to understand what clients may expect from counseling, to clarify our own expectations of the client and therapist role, and to modify it if need be to meet client goals. We strongly urge psychologists to seek consultation with others and to be on culturally diverse consultation teams to help identify when traditional interventions are not appropriate and how they might be modified. As we noted earlier, for many ethnoracial minority clients, family and extended networks are very important, as is the role of spirituality. We encourage therapists to examine ways to incorporate an understanding of those roles into therapy. Finally, consistent with our argument in chapter 7 that psychologists are strongly encouraged to be advocates for change, we are encouraging psychologists to examine whether there are ways to advocate for our clients.

Summary

This chapter focused on developing culturally competent psychological practice. We believe there is a moral imperative for all psychologists to develop cultural competence, but there is an additional pragmatic reality. In a world that is increasingly culturally diverse, ethnoracial minority clients are not seeking treatment. If we psychologists are competent to only work with White clients, we will have a shrinking client pool. The U.S. Surgeon General's report (USDHHS, 2001) showed that ethnoracial minority clients are clearly in need of psychological services. Yet, they are either not seeking treatment for psychological distress or do not stay in treatment long enough for it to be effective, in part because they do not trust the cultural competence of their therapist. We psychologists need to approach each client with an understanding of the role that the client's cultural context may play in his or her problems, to use culturally appropriate assessments, and to learn how to adapt our interventions to be culturally appropriate.

Implications for Psychologists as Educators 5

I entered the classroom with the conviction that it was crucial for me and every other student to be an active participant, not a passive consumer . . . [a conception of] education as the practice of freedom . . . education that connects the will to know with the will to become. Learning is a place where paradise can be created.

—hooks, 1994

Guideline 3: As educators, psychologists are encouraged to employ the constructs of multiculturalism and diversity in psychological education.[1]

Competency Statements

Psychologists who use the constructs of "multiculturalism" and "diversity" in psychological education will be able to demonstrate

- knowledge about different learning models and approaches to teaching from multiple cultural perspectives,
- knowledge of how to incorporate statements of philosophy and principles in course syllabi,
- knowledge of how to design a culture-centered curriculum that is thematic to an educational program,
- knowledge of how to anticipate a range of emotional reactions in students and be prepared to understand and facilitate respectful discussion and disagreement, and
- knowledge of the research findings about the effects of multicultural counseling and psychology coursework.

---

[1]Cited in "Guidelines on Multicultural Education, Training, Research, Practice, and Organizational Change for Psychologists," American Psychological Association (APA; 2003, p. 386; see also APA Web site version at http://www.apa.org/pi/multiculturalguidelines/).

Overview

In this chapter, we present a rationale for a culture-centered approach to psychological education and training, and we apply the material discussed in chapters 2 and 3 first to infusing a culture-centered perspective into an educational program in psychology, present critical elements of a culture-centered educational program, and then discuss teaching strategies within the classroom. Thus, we hope to discuss the implementation of Guideline 3 from both a broad, overarching perspective of the entire program from recruitment to evaluation of students, as well as the narrower topic of what we do as teachers and trainers within our classrooms to incorporate strategies to reach students with a variety of learning styles and differing cultural values.

Rationale

Infusing a culture-centered approach into education and training has been a goal for many institutions and programs over the past 30 years (Constantine, Ladany, Inman, & Ponterotto, 1996; Lee et al., 1999; McDowell, Fang, Brownlee, Young, & Khanna, 2002; Ponterotto, 1997; Quintana & Bernal, 1995; Rogers, Hoffman, & Wade, 1998). This greater focus on culture-centered educational practices has been based on two fundamental motivational influences. The first influence is an increasingly held belief that the best practitioners, researchers, and educators are products of a culture-centered approach and that indeed, students must be prepared to function in a culturally competent manner once they graduate. By the same token, educators are increasingly coming to believe that traditional models of instruction have disproportionately favored White, middle-class students and that different strategies and approaches to learning are needed to effectively reach culturally heterogeneous student groups.

The few empirical studies on the effectiveness of a culture-centered approach to education have documented an increase in students' self-awareness (Achenbach & Arthur, 2002; S. P. Brown, Parham, & Yonker, 1996), knowledge and skills in multicultural counseling (Manese, Wu, & Nepomuceno, 2001), and an increase in their therapeutic competence (D'Andrea, Daniels, & Heck, 1991; Pope-Davis & Ottavi, 1994). Other studies have found cultural differences in learning style preferences (e.g., Dunn, Griggs, & Price, 1993; Park, 2001), suggesting that less traditional teaching strategies are necessary to respond to those differences. Abreu

(2001), Findlay and Stephan (2000), and Steele (1997) suggested that a culture-centered approach to education may also help to counteract the types of automatic categorization and stereotyping described in chapters 2 and 3.

The second, much more implicit, influence in developing culture-centered educational programs is an increasing sense that institutions of higher learning are responsible for creating an environment that is inclusive and committed to valuing diversity (Allen, n.d.). M. T. Brown (2004) suggested that institutions of higher education must take a leadership role in helping society cope with challenges of increasing ethnoracial diversity. However, as Hurtado, Carter, and Kardia (1998) noted, although a number of institutions are assessing the climate of tolerance on campus, many are not actively taking steps to disseminate the findings from those surveys, and changes are not always institutionalized (Reid & Radhakrishnan, 2003). But, although institutions may be lagging on creating effective change mechanisms, psychology-accrediting bodies, state licensing boards, and in one case, the California Department of Education, have mandated that programs and institutions attend to issues of diversity in the educational setting.

Infusing a Multiculturally Centered Perspective Into Psychological Curricula

The 1973 Vail Conference was one of the first times that focusing on a client's cultural background was explicitly addressed; conference recommendations included an ethical imperative to have knowledge about cultural differences, as well as the skills to work with culturally diverse clients (Korman, 1974). Educational programs in psychology began to scramble to incorporate a course in multicultural counseling, and in 1982, two studies showed some limited progress in training culturally competent applied psychologists. A study conducted by the American Psychological Association (APA; Bernal & Padilla, 1982) indicated that only 4% of psychology programs had a required course on assessment of minorities, and only 17% had an elective course available. Bernal and Padilla (1982) found that, of the 76 accredited clinical psychology programs responding (out of a possible 106), 31 programs had at least one multicultural counseling course. In a follow-up study a decade later (Bernal & Castro, 1994), 104 programs responded, and 64 had a multicultural counseling or assessment course, but only 13% required students to take it. Thus, training programs were strongly encouraged to

EXHIBIT 5.1

Critical Elements of a Multiculturally Infused Psychology Curriculum

1. Explicitly state a commitment to diversity and the philosophy of the program.
2. Actively make an effort to recruit and graduate students from diverse populations.
3. Actively make an effort to recruit and retain a diverse faculty.
4. Make efforts to make the admissions process fair and equitable.
5. Ensure that students gain awareness of their own cultural values and biases, knowledge of other groups, and skills to work with diverse populations.
6. Examine all courses for infusion of a culture-centered approach throughout the curriculum.
7. Evaluate students on their cultural competence at least annually.

develop a course in multicultural counseling or services. Some heeded the call: Lee et al. (1999) found that internship sites had infused multicultural training into internship training.

In 2005, over a decade after Bernal and Castro's (1994) follow-up work, the debate is no longer focused on whether to have a single course on multicultural counseling and assessment but rather on how to effectively infuse a culture-centered perspective throughout the entire curriculum and program. Arredondo and Arciniega (2001) suggested that training programs are learning environments in which students gain an appreciation for, commitment to, and skill base to become culturally competent. Speight, Thomas, Kennel, and Anderson (1995) asked experts to identify the critical components of multicultural programs, finding that infusion of multicultural issues throughout the curriculum was the most frequently cited component. Diversity of students and of faculty were next, and experts also advocated for a single course in addition to an infusion across the curriculum. Those evaluating academic programs also noted that the philosophy of the program, a multicultural curriculum, and faculty with multicultural expertise were critical in demonstrating cultural competence.

In other words, developing culturally competent students is most likely to occur in a training program that has a focus on, and demonstrates sensitivity to, culture in all elements of the program—from statement of mission, to recruiting a diverse student and faculty group, to curriculum and evaluations. These critical elements are listed in Exhibit 5.1 and are described in more detail next.

EXPLICITLY STATE A COMMITMENT TO DIVERSITY AND THE PHILOSOPHY OF THE PROGRAM

Perhaps the most critical initial step of multicultural infusion is to ensure that the entire faculty is committed to pursuit of such a goal. Often the first challenge of a program is to engage all other faculty, who may be resistant to change or fearful of engaging in cultural self-reflection and in pursuing this as a program goal. Once faculty have jointly agreed to the goal, it is important for them to explicitly state a philosophy valuing cultural diversity and express a commitment to training students to be culturally competent. For example, Seton Hall University's counseling psychology program handbook and brochure indicate the program's commitment to training multiculturally sensitive and competent professionals and goes on to note that this is done through coursework, practicums, proseminars, and interactions with faculty.

ACTIVELY MAKE AN EFFORT TO RECRUIT AND GRADUATE STUDENTS FROM DIVERSE POPULATIONS

This effort begins with application and recruitment materials that have been found to be effective in recruiting students of color. Bidell, Turner, and Casas (2002) found that the most effective materials include the program's philosophy statement and commitment to diversity and nondiscrimination, information on financial aid, and evidence of a commitment to training in diversity (e.g., courses, faculty research interests). The American Psychological Association (APA) Commission on Ethnic Minority Recruitment, Retention, and Training in Psychology (CEMRRAT) Work Group on Student Recruitment (1998) also suggested that effective recruitment packets are ones that are well organized, reviewed for clarity of the application and admissions process, and include demographic information about the students and faculty in the program. They also recommend including a community resource guide geared toward interests and needs of ethnic minority students, and finally, they recommend that the packet be personally addressed to the prospective student.

ACTIVELY MAKE AN EFFORT TO RECRUIT AND RETAIN A DIVERSE FACULTY

A racially and ethnically diverse faculty is critical to a culture-centered educational program (APA, 1996a; Kirkpatrick, 2001). As noted by Antonio (2002), faculty of color

EXHIBIT 5.2

Recruiting Racially/Ethnically Diverse Faculty

1. Recognize the value of non-academic experiences.
2. Include area minority professionals on the search committee.
3. Utilize minority media in recruitment campaigns (e.g., journals targeting ethnoracial populations).
4. Recruit outside academia.
5. Keep candidate pools open until minority applicants are found.
6. Maintain communication with traditionally ethnically focused colleges and universities.
7. Include ethnoracial minority group members on the interview schedule.
8. Target hiring outside the normal process (Smith et al., 2004).
9. Show evidence of long-range programs encouraging minority and women students.
10. Show evidence of institutional commitment from the campus and college levels.
11. Create an intern or postdoctoral program for students of color who can then move into faculty positions.
12. Provide opportunities for mentoring.

provide students with diverse role models, assist in providing more effective mentoring to minority students, are supportive of minority-related and other areas of nontraditional areas of scholarship, and give minorities a greater voice in the governance of the nation's colleges and universities. (p. 583)

Colby and Foote (1995) compiled a number of strategies for recruiting a diverse faculty; these are outlined in Exhibit 5.2. In addition, a CEMRRAT (APA, 1998) guide for women and ethnic minorities considering a career in academia suggested that academic candidates assess the institutions' commitment to diversity (evident in statements of mission, initiatives, policies, and programs), the proportion of other faculty members who are members of ethnoracial minorities, the number of ethnoracial minority members who are in administration (and type of position held), and whether public statements made by administration show evidence of commitment to diversity. Faculty in a program committed to recruiting a diverse faculty pool would do well not only to use strategies in Exhibit 5.2 but also to evaluate their own institution relative to its commitment to diversity. Smith, Turner, Osei-Kofi, and Richards (2004) recommended a number of strategies for successful recruiting of a culturally diverse faculty, suggesting that the best method is a targeted hire. A CEMRRAT (APA, 1996b) report suggested that programs evaluate their readiness to hire minority faculty, including clarifying the expectations the program has for the faculty member and evaluating the program's readiness to value diversity and to create a climate of support for cultural diversity in teaching and research. CEMRRAT guidelines for effective recruitment begin with position announcements that convey an institutional commitment to diversity, using a diversity advocate during the screening process to ensure deliberate attention is paid to issues of fairness and equity, and creating ongoing activities to be alert to the possibility of recruiting faculty of color for future positions.

MAKE EFFORTS TO MAKE THE ADMISSIONS PROCESS FAIR AND EQUITABLE

This is critical to meet the legal requirements that admissions is not race based; thus, each individual is treated fairly and equitably. But it is also critical that the process is transparent and appears fair and equitable. For example, the University of Nebraska has an Ethnic Minority Affairs Committee (EMAC) in the Department of Educational Psychology, composed of ethnic minority students and faculty; EMAC has been functioning for over 30 years. Ethnic minority applicants are invited to have their applications reviewed first by EMAC, which promises to bring applications to the faculty admissions committee for consideration. Although no guarantees are made that ethnic minority students will receive special consideration, this additional step is a valued part of the process for both current ethnic minority students and ethnic minority applicants.

ENSURE THAT STUDENTS GAIN AWARENESS OF THEIR OWN CULTURAL VALUES AND BIASES, KNOWLEDGE OF OTHER GROUPS, AND SKILLS TO WORK WITH DIVERSE POPULATIONS

This may include a dedicated course in which students first gain awareness and exposure to the knowledge base. Such a course appears to be the primary vehicle for transmission of multicultural competence (Priester, Jackson-Bailey, Jones, Jordan, & Metz, 2004). In a study of accredited counseling psychology programs, all respondents (82% of the 67 programs) had at least one course dedicated to multicultural awareness. Of those 55 programs, 43% emphasized self-awareness activities, 82% emphasized knowledge of other groups, and only 13% emphasized skill development. Although skill development must, of necessity, come after awareness and knowledge of self and other groups, multicultural competence must include a focus on developing skills to work with diverse populations, including role playing and encouraging students to seek practicum experiences in which they will gain exposure to a diverse client population (and in which they will have good supervision for their

EXHIBIT 5.3

Questions for Culture-Centered Instruction

1. Are the objectives for the course culture-centered?
2. Are the topics covered in the course inclusive of ethnoracial diversity?
3. Does the curriculum include non-Western perspectives?
4. Are the readings for the course appropriately inclusive and diverse?
5. Are the assignments geared toward encouraging students to learn about the course content from diverse perspectives?
6. Does the evaluation for the course appear to include accountability for knowledge or skills related to cultural diversity?

new skill development; Constantine, 2001; McCreary & Walker, 2001; Sevig & Etzkorn, 2001).

EXAMINE ALL COURSES FOR INFUSION OF A CULTURE-CENTERED APPROACH THROUGHOUT THE CURRICULUM

This includes the foundational courses in addition to the skills-based courses involved in clinical training. Often a multicultural audit done in conjunction with a self-study for accreditation or university program reviews provides a good opportunity for programs to evaluate syllabi for courses across the curriculum. Evaluation questions are included in Exhibit 5.3.

EVALUATE STUDENTS ON THEIR CULTURAL COMPETENCE AT LEAST ANNUALLY

Programs that explicitly hold students accountable for cultural competence communicate the value of that competence to students. Evaluation mechanisms may include asking students to comment on the steps they have taken to increase cultural competence during the year, asking supervisors to comment on students' growth in cultural competence, or evaluating students on a standardized assessment of multicultural competence.

Teaching Strategies for a Multiculturally Centered Approach

The previous section discussed incorporating a culture-centered focus into an entire curriculum; it is also important to discuss what occurs in individual classrooms. Traditional methods of instruction in graduate programs of psychology have featured an instructor who determines the material to be covered, creates a syllabus that covers that material, and then delivers it primarily via lectures. Students come prepared to listen and take notes, and they expect to be fairly passive during the class time. Evaluation of their work in the class usually includes a paper at the end of the course, with at least one, if not two, exams during the semester and a final at the end of the course. The work done during class is expected to be done individually, rather than in a group, and grading is often done on a curve. The method of instruction, in other words, is focused on the material to be covered, rather than on the student learning the material, and students who do well are able to thrive in a competitive environment.

This traditional model of instruction worked well if classes were homogeneous with regard to learning style and the professor's views of the material to be covered were unquestioned. But, traditional models of instruction work less well in heterogeneous classrooms, including culturally heterogeneous classrooms and classrooms in which students have different learning styles and have begun to question the professor's perspective about the focus of the material being covered. Students may also have different values about competition. For example, students from cultures that place higher value on collectivism (Hofstede & McCrae, 2004; Triandis, 2001; Triandis & Suh, 2002) with its focus on group goals rather than on individual goals (e.g., traditional African American, Latino, Asian American, and Native American cultures) may feel uncomfortable with an emphasis on competition that highlights a single individual's achievement. Students with a high value on collectivism may shy away from competition and do less well in this environment, but they may thrive in more cooperative learning situations.

A series of focus groups with students conducted at the University of Michigan (Chesler, Wilson, & Malani, 1993) highlighted the negative effect of traditional models of instruction on students of color. When asked if they were ever uncomfortable with assumptions made in class or if they felt that faculty could make the material more meaningful, students identified several areas of concern: their feeling that faculty had low expectations of them, lacked time for students, lacked an understanding that students of color are different from White students, had expectations that all members of an ethnoracial minority group are alike, expected them to be a spokesperson for their ethnic group, excluded them from the curriculum and classroom interaction, and often seemed uncomfortable with them. Although some of these concerns may be related to cultural insensitivity or covert racism, they also voiced barriers to learning that focused on teaching strategies. For example, they expressed concerns that teachers used examples that were primarily geared to European American culture and at times skipped over them when asking for comments. They also noted that teachers did not acknowledge that perspectives or theories from other cultural groups may inform the content under discussion.

The concerns outlined by the students in these groups led to a series of workshops with faculty at the University of Michigan, which resulted in several recommendations (Chesler et al., 1993). Recommendations focused on curriculum and teaching strategies as well as on classroom environment. The first area included suggestions that faculty make classroom content and pedagogy more inclusive, and that the curriculum should represent diverse perspectives and traditions, that pedagogical strategies more actively engage students rather than expect them to be passive recipients of information. The second area focused on suggestions that faculty create a safe and inclusive environment for all students, treat all students as individuals, and learn how to manage controversial and emotional discussions. Strategies in these two areas are discussed more fully in the next section.

CURRICULUM DEVELOPMENT AND PEDAGOGICAL STRATEGIES

Developing a culture-centered approach to teaching includes knowing one's own biases and having some knowledge about the ways that groups differ, as discussed in chapters 2 and 3. It also includes having knowledge about the different ways that individuals prefer to learn. Differences in learning styles are related to the ways that students process and apply information and have been found to differ across cultures (Harkness & Keefer, 2000; Park, 2001). There are multiple ways to designate learning styles, and a comprehensive review of learning style differences is beyond the scope of this book; readers are referred to Boyd, Hunt, Kandell, and Lucas (2003); Cassidy (2004); Evans (2004); and Renzulli and Dai (2001). However, instructors are encouraged to consider that the students may have different preferences for learning strategies, for example, that students may learn best visually, verbally, aurally, actively, or reflectively, and that these preferences may differ by culture of origin. Students who are visual learners learn best by graphs, videos, and information presented on a board or projector; verbal learners learn best by listening to lectures; aural learners need to hear material said out loud to learn it; active learners learn best by engagement in an activity or discussion; and reflective learners learn best by introspection. Because the students in a class may represent a variety of learning styles, regardless of cultural identity, teachers will be most effective if they include a variety of pedagogical strategies and approaches (Saunders & Kardia, n.d.).

EXHIBIT 5.4

Questions to Ask in Designing a Course

1. Examples and anecdotes: Are the examples I'm using understood by all groups in class? Am I gender and culture fair in the examples I'm using? Have I reviewed my case examples, anecdotes, and illustrations to make sure they are understood by all?
2. Teaching strategies: Am I including a variety of strategies in my class to reach multiple types of learners? Are there additional ways I could teach the material that would encompass more cooperative, or collectivistic, activities?
3. Grading procedures: Are my grading procedures flexible to maximize student preferences for learning? Do they allow students to adequately demonstrate their comprehension of the material? Are the grading criteria explained thoroughly in the syllabus and have I ensured that all students are treated fairly?
4. Classroom environment: Have I set ground rules that help to create an environment that is safe? Do I have strategies to handle somewhat controversial topics? Do I have ideas of how to handle resistance, should that occur?

A multiculturally centered approach to teaching encompasses the content of the course, the strategies used to deliver that content, and the ways that students are evaluated on the material. Questions that we may ask ourselves as teachers designing a course are outlined in Exhibit 5.4; these topics are discussed more fully next.

In designing the content of the course, teachers are encouraged to develop a syllabus that has multiple perspectives on the topic. As Lehman, Chiu, and Schaller (2004) noted, "Psychological processes influence culture. Culture influences psychological processes" (p. 690). Most areas of psychology can be informed by cross-cultural and cross-ethnic comparisons, and we teachers are encouraged to include those varying perspectives in our creation of the course as well as in the readings assigned for the course. One of the areas that we are encouraged to avoid is using examples from our own referent point. For example, we are encouraged to use sports analogies represented by both men and women or to use examples from popular culture that are accessed by many groups and social classes. Teachers might want to think through examples and illustrative points to make sure that students of all cultures would be likely to have background in the material.

Strategies that reach different types of learners were briefly discussed previously and include small discussion groups, varying lecture with classroom discussion, using exercises in class, and using visual materials and handouts. Jones (2004) recommended carefully balancing academic content with instructional process and encouraged the use of visual aids, group work, and building on what students know. Halpern (2004) recommended the use of cooperative learning to foster students' active learning, noting that cooperative learning shifts learning from the teacher to the student. She cited six critical ingredients for successful cooperative learning: (a) positive interdependence among students, in which students' success depends on the other members of the group; (b) individual accountability, so that student learning is assessed individually; (c) appropriate assignment to groups, ensuring heterogeneity within groups; (d) the teacher as a facilitator of group processes; (e) attention to students' social skills, so ground rules are set about respect and expectations of treatment of others in the class; and (f) cognitive principles applied to this type of learning, including increased time on task, more immediate feedback, modeling thinking and learning, and connecting knowledge structures for students. Her teaching tips include a number of tips to incorporate cooperative learning in different types of classes. For example, for a large lecture class, she recommends stopping in the middle and asking students to summarize to another student, who then gives feedback on his or her comprehension. For a statistics class, she suggests small-group problem solving, and for an applied psychology class, she suggests presenting an applied problem and asking students to brainstorm three questions to ask about the problem to guide their solution of that problem. McGlynn (1999) suggested that cooperative learning environments may work particularly well with students from collectivist cultures (e.g., Hispanic/Latino, African American, Asian American cultures), because they foster harmony in the classroom and reduce prejudice among groups.

Experiential activities have also been recommended as pedagogical strategies, particularly in the areas of clinical skills. In these activities, students are expected to engage in the experience of interacting with individuals from culturally different groups, either directly or vicariously. These may include using videos, role playing, conducting cross-cultural interviews, writing cultural autobiographies, discussing case examples or dilemmas (Dadeghi, Fischer, & House, 2003), tracking cultural genograms (Keiley et al., 2002), or engaging in exercises to clarify values (Achenbach & Arthur, 2002; Arthur & Achenbach, 2002; Diaz-Lázaro & Cohen, 2001; Evans & Larrabee, 2002). Kim and Lyons (2003) suggested an additional type of experiential activity, advocating for the use of games in multicultural counseling training. They cited a number of specific games for use in increasing students' culture-centered attitudes, knowledge, and skills (e.g., use of a quiz show format, brainstorming interpretations of nonverbal behavior).

The final component in a multiculturally centered approach to teaching is evaluation of student learning. As noted previously, Halpern (2004) recommended that students be held individually accountable for their knowledge, suggesting that student assignments and contributions are graded separately. Other scholars recommend a more flexible approach to grading, allowing students to choose which aspects of the required assignments to count. This allows a reserved student to put more emphasis on exams or papers, and a test-anxious student to put more emphasis on participation or papers. It also allows students to be able to demonstrate their comprehension and synthesis of the material in a variety of ways (Center for Teaching and Learning, University of North Carolina at Chapel Hill [CTL-UNC], 1997). Regardless of the approach, it is critical that grading criteria are clearly explained and adhered to fairly.

SAFE AND INCLUSIVE ENVIRONMENT

The second area that is recommended for teachers is creating a safe environment for all students, one in which they feel respected, included, and protected. It would be a rare teacher who would not ascribe to the value of the classroom as a safe environment for learning, but we are also suggesting that it is the teacher's responsibility to actively create this environment. This includes getting to know students as individuals, explicitly making it acceptable to express differing viewpoints in class, reminding students to address other students' ideas rather than attacking them personally, and making classroom norms explicit (CTL-UNC, 1997). The McGraw-Hill Multicultural Supersite (Gorski, 2003) has a list of ground rules that teachers may discuss with our classes. These include the following: respect others when they are talking, speak from your own experience, challenge each other respectfully, participate to your fullest ability, and note that the goal is not to agree but to discuss and hear different perspectives. Depending on the class topic or area, teachers may also want to ask students to respect other students' confidentiality and remind students to share only what they are comfortable sharing. Finally, it is helpful for teachers to note at the outset that they reserve the right to call on students as well as to limit the contributions of some students to give everyone an equal opportunity to contribute.

There are also some things to avoid in creating a safe environment (CTL-UNC, 1997). Do not, for example, expect one student, such as an ethnoracial minority student or a woman (or a man) to speak for a whole group. Do not expect that students of color will be knowledgeable about race or racism, but also do not assume they will automatically be uncomfortable discussing these topics. Do not let harmful or racist statements pass without comment; one way to address such comments is to acknowledge that some might find the statement or comment offensive and ask the students to examine the assumptions behind such a statement. Do not allow other students to scapegoat one student or a particular viewpoint. Finally, do not allow students to avoid participation; teachers may invite participation or create opportunities for students to participate in smaller groups.

The last area for creating and maintaining a safe classroom environment is perhaps the most difficult of all: Dealing with resistance and with the emotional reactions to discussions of race and culture. Poe (2004) outlined three challenges to teaching controversial topics: (a) loss of composure on the part of the teacher, (b) inappropriate self-disclosure by students, and (c) opinions expressed as fact. Poe recommended letting students know at the beginning of the course that sensitive topics may be discussed, giving students an informed choice of remaining in the class. She also recommended that instructors recall that their role is to help students learn and grow in their knowledge and comprehension of the material but are not in the role of group or individual therapists. There is a difference between engaging a class in a challenging discussion that evokes emotional reactions and helping an individual student work through a personal problem or concern.

Additional strategies may include asking students to step back from a heated exchange, asking them to reflect on it and what they have learned and how the discussion may reflect societal perspectives (Derek Bok Center for Teaching and Learning, 2004). The Derek Bok Center for Teaching and Learning (2004) also suggested that teachers explicitly recognize and address students' fears about conflict and their comfort level with emotional discourse. Jackson (1999) suggested reminding students that comfort with issues of diversity is developmental and thus, they will vary in that comfort level.

A final and often difficult aspect of explicitly addressing race and culture in the classroom is handling resistant students; resistance may come from White students (Abreu, 2001; Utsey & Gernat, 2002; Utsey, McCarthy, Eukanks, & Adrian, 2002); it may also come from students of color (Jackson, 1999). Some of the reasons for this resistance were discussed in chapter 2. Ridley and Thompson (1999) provided an extensive discussion of sources of resistance and reactions to resistance, and they end their chapter with several recommendations. One recommendation is to identify resistance in terms of student behavior (change-opposing or change-promoting) and the outcomes of that behavior (counterproductive or constructive). Change-opposing behavior that is counterproductive is the easiest to spot: Students overtly resist engaging in activities, verbally protest participation in activities, or openly challenge the value of multiculturally focused education. Change-promoting behavior that is counterproductive is covert and is thus less easy to see, but indicates lack of commitment to change or to engage in the process of training. Resistance is subtle. More constructive behaviors may be change-opposing (evident in overt protests) or change-promoting, in which the student is compliant with the training process.

Additional recommendations include directly confronting the resistance, encouraging the trainer to not react defensively, and incorporating exercises that help students to identify the source of their resistance. At times, asking the students to read materials and providing didactic instruction about race, prejudice, and analysis of power may help students to have an intellectual framework into which they can place their feelings of resistance. Following the didactic portion with experiential exercises may allow students to engage in those exercises more freely. For example, if an undergraduate student is taking an introductory course in psychology, naiveté to a multiculturally diverse world may appear as resistant behavior. A student may not be aware of the relevance of certain issues or that such concerns exist outside their personal frame of reference. An instructor's presentation of the material is essential to cultivate an understanding of certain multicultural principles. Internalizing these principles or integrating them into a larger scope of knowledge and practice may not be appropriate at this level of learning. Developing awareness is the goal for students new to multicultural competencies, which gives them a foundation to build upon and use. A graduate student taking a course on social psychology, on the other hand, has more experience with which to question and challenge his or her feelings of resistance to issues of culture and race. Encouraging students at the more advanced levels of learning to be aware and accountable for their own interpretation and internalization of material enhances their training process and widens the scope of their learning lens. If they are encouraged to see how their reaction to multicultural issues affects their practice, they can develop an understanding of the link between the information they learn and the practical application of that knowledge. For example, a graduate student in a social psychology class can be asked to discuss the contact hypothesis in the theoretical sense from literature in the social psychology class. This can be followed by an exercise that would entail this student to integrate this theory in hypothetical situations, for example, in answers to questions such as "How could this theory have been used in conflict resolution strategies following the Los Angeles riots of 1992?" or, "If a school is having racial tensions on campus, how could this theory be integrated to alleviate hostilities?" By encouraging students to personalize their knowledge of racial or cultural issues, they, along with the instructor, can explicitly address resistance.

Summary

This chapter focused on applying awareness of self and awareness of other groups to the educational setting. We discussed the rationale for a culture-centered approach to education and training, the most critical of which is that graduates from multiculturally focused programs are more effective practitioners, researchers, teachers, and agents of change. We also discussed different approaches to teaching from multiple cultural perspectives, and we outlined the various components in an educational program that can be addressed from a culture-centered perspective. We also encouraged teachers to adapt various pedagogical styles and techniques to accommodate differences among their students. Finally, we discussed various ways of handling student resistance.

Implications for Psychologists as Researchers

6

*Aristotle maintained that women have fewer teeth than men;
although he was twice married, it never occurred to him to verify this
statement by examining his wives' mouths.*
  —Bertrand Russell, *Impact of Science on Society*

*Guideline 4: Culturally sensitive psychological researchers are
encouraged to recognize the importance of conducting culture-centered
and ethical psychological research among persons from ethnic,
linguistic, and racial minority backgrounds.*[1]

Competency Statements

Psychologists who use the constructs of "multiculturalism" and "diversity" in psychological research will be able to demonstrate

- ability to examine their own biases in developing research questions;
- knowledge of the way race and gender have been dealt with throughout the history of psychological research;
- understanding of the consequences of not incorporating culture as a central variable in psychological research;
- understanding the need to incorporate cultural context into research questions; and
- knowledge of the role of cultural context in research design, assessment, and interpretation of data.

---

[1]Cited in "Guidelines on Multicultural Education, Training, Research, Practice, and Organizational Change for Psychologists," American Psychological Association (APA; 2003, p. 388; see also APA Web site version at http://www.apa.org/pi/multiculturalguidelines/).

Overview: Race–Ethnicity and Psychological Research

The role of culture, race, and ethnicity in psychological research has grown over the past several decades. Early psychologists either ignored culture, assuming that all individuals were the same, regardless of gender or race, or they believed that racial differences were as a result of a deficit of those who were not White (or men). As examples of these tendencies, consider two abstracts from early studies. In 1915, Kelley's abstract stated that he

> investigated the possible correlation between grades received in different years and the connection between poor scholastic standing and withdrawal from university. The grades of 100 students who entered university after graduating from the high school were studied . . . only 23 freshmen completed their university studies. About 22 per cent elimination was attributed to causes other than failure. (p. 365)

As another example, in 1919, Bache reported

> RT [response time] increases with evolution, so that the RT of superior races is higher than that of inferior ones, with the support of results from an experiment on 34 Whites, Blacks, and Red Indians (aged 14–38 yrs) . . . lower RTs in Blacks imply inferiority of race, and lower RTs in women are in accordance with the higher brain development of men. (p. 475)

The race and sex of the subjects were not variables of interest in Kelley's study, and indeed were not mentioned in the article; clearly the assumption is that the results would hold for all subjects, even though "causes other than failure" may be different for different groups. By comparison, the interpretations from Bache's study are that women and minorities are innately inferior to White men, a conclusion that was a product of the context of the early 20th century. Deficit orientations continued to dominate psychology's examination of racial differences until the end of the 20th century, although the conclusions began to be couched in terms of "cultural deficit," "cultural impoverishment," or "cultural disadvantage," all terms used to connote that differences were a result of something lacking within ethnoracial minority communities. White, usually middle-class, men were used to define normal behavior, and any behavior that differed from such normal behavior was either deviant or less desirable.

In the 1970s and early 1980s, women began to argue that current psychological research was biased against women. Schwabacher (1972) and Reardon and Prescott (1977) documented the very few studies that reported the gender of participants, and Gilligan (1977) challenged no-tions of stages of moral development as not descriptive of women's experiences. Broverman, Vogel, Broverman, Clarkson, and Rosenkranz (1972) reported their now-famous findings that descriptions of mentally healthy adults and mentally healthy men were the same whereas descriptions of mentally healthy women were viewed as mentally unhealthy adults, and Keller (1982) wrote about the masculine bias that was inherently embedded in objective scientific methods.

Early multicultural researchers (Korchin, 1980; D. W. Sue, 1983) also began to voice concern about a White bias in research. Guthrie (1976) wrote a book about his experiences as an African American psychologist, titled *Even the Rat Was White*. Katz (1985) delineated the White values embedded in counseling and therapy and encouraged researchers to explicitly understand how their cultural perspectives and values shaped their work. D. W. Sue and Sue (1977) wrote their first of many articles exhorting the counseling field to be more culturally competent, and they urged the field to conduct more culturally appropriate research as well.

Thus, feminists and ethnoracial activists advocated that science be more inclusive and questioned the validity of scientific results at a time in the United States when many traditional concepts were being questioned. The outcome of their activism was twofold. First, more and more journal editors insisted on reporting the gender and racial makeup of participants in studies, so it became clearer to whom the results generalized. Second, researchers began to statistically control for sex and race as nuisance variables, rather than as an intrinsic part of the research question.

Concerns began to arise about these practices, though. First, it became clear that even though journal editors were requiring authors to report sample characteristics, the vast majority of study participants were White, middle-class students, and researchers continued to assume that results applied to all populations. Researchers also failed to consider, or even to assess, the many differences within ethnoracial groups that may be due to region of the country, language, socioeconomic status, education, and national origin. Thus they ignored differences among those who emigrated from Cuba and those who emigrated from Mexico, or differences between those African Americans who were descendants of slaves, those who emigrated from Africa, and those who were originally from Caribbean islands. Third, statistical control of race or gender does not allow a researcher to incorporate culture as a central variable. The result is that behavior is inappropriately interpreted or is too often identified as pathological. Many have warned psychologists that by not incorporating culture into their research, they are at risk of perpetuating harm (G. C. N. Hall, 2001; Rogler, 1999; D. W. Sue et al., 1998; D. W. Sue & Sue, 1999). The Council of National Psychological Associations for the Advancement of Ethnic Minority Interests (CNPAAEMI) noted that psychology as a whole has been based on Western European assumptions and perspectives and that "the effects of such biases have, at times, been detrimental to the diverse needs of the populations we serve and the public interest and have compromised our ability to accurately understand the people that we serve" (2000, p. 1).

As an example of the possible dangers inherent in not incorporating a culture-centered perspective, consider a study conducted by Combs, Penn, and Fenigstein (2002). They examined ethnic group differences in levels of paranoia and subclinical paranoia, self-esteem, trust, depression, fear, and social anxiety. They found ethnic group differences on paranoia, with African Americans reporting higher levels of paranoia and higher levels of social anxiety. Not incorporating a culture-centered perspective might lead a researcher to conclude a high level of psychopathology in the African American sample. Combs et al. questioned, however, whether the elevated scales may have been the result of mistrust or wariness due to discrimination and racism, and they concluded that different standards need to be applied for African Americans to conclude that paranoia is pathological.

In this chapter, we present a rationale for explicitly including cultural and linguistic diversity in psychological research. We argue that rather than statistically controlling for diversity as a nuisance variable, good psychological science is best informed by questions framed by cultural context. Thus, psychological researchers are encouraged to be grounded in the empirical and conceptual literature on the ways that culture influences the variables under investigation, as well as psychological and social science research traditions and skills. We discuss four aspects: research assumptions and design, assessment, analysis, and dissemination. We use Case Vignettes 1 and 2 as we discuss each area.

Case Vignette 1: Marlene

Marlene, a doctoral student in a clinical psychology program, is interested in conducting her dissertation on treatment effectiveness of cognitive–behavioral therapy for anxiety and depression. She has access to a large clinical population, receives approval from her university review board, and proceeds to conduct her study. She decides to assess anxiety and depression with standardized surveys before and after treatment and to evaluate treatment effectiveness by the decrease in the scores on the instruments. She collects demographic information on her participants and finds that at the start of treatment, 60% are women but that women are less likely to finish treatment than men (65% of the final sample are men). She also finds that 70% of the participants seeking treatment (i.e., available at pretest) for depression and anxiety are European American, with 12% African American, 12% Hispanic/Latino, 2% Asian American, and 4% Native American, but her final sample is 90% European American.

Case Vignette 2: Julia

Julia is a doctoral student in a counseling psychology program, located in a large urban setting. She has completed a practicum in a community-based counseling center with a clientele diverse in race, cultural backgrounds, sexual orientation, socioeconomic status, and religious affiliation. She notices that even though the services at the center are modeled on a 50-minute hour, some of her clients are uncomfortable sitting in one chair talking to her for an hour, some clients clearly want to stay longer than an hour, and others complain that talking will not help their problems and ask her to do something more concrete to help them. These differences in client preference appear to be related to race or ethnicity. She develops an idea for a dissertation on effective treatment paradigms that differ with culture-centered preferences for therapeutic modalities. She talks with the counseling center's director about her ideas, and he is eager to help her with her study because he is also concerned with cultural differences in treatment maintenance.

Research Assumptions and Design

RESEARCH ASSUMPTIONS

We discussed earlier the assumptions underlying much of psychological research throughout the 20th century, which shifted from cultural inferiority, to cultural deficit, to statistical control, and ultimately, we hope, to culture as a central variable of interest. It is clear, however, that researchers' worldviews and the assumptions they make strongly affect the way that culture is treated in psychological science. Exhibit 6.1 outlines some of the questions that researchers can ask themselves as they begin a research project.

Although it may seem preposterous to psychologists in the 21st century, assumptions of inferiority of non-Whites continued until the end of the 20th century. For example, Herrnstein and Murray's (1994) contro-

EXHIBIT 6.1

Checking Your Research Assumptions

Identify two research questions you have. Answer the following questions about those ideas:

■ How did you generate your research question?
■ How would you classify your questions (descriptive, difference, or relationship)?
■ What cultural assumptions are inherent in your questions?
■ What might be cultural limitations of your questions?
■ What do you already know about theoretical frameworks that influence your research question?
■ How might theoretical frameworks from other cultural groups influence your research question?
■ How might your research question be of benefit to ethnoracial minority communities?
■ How can you make your research findings generalizable to more than one population?
■ What might be particular concerns you would have to ensure external validity for your findings (e.g., what may be concerns of sampling beyond more than one cultural group)?

versial book *The Bell Curve* purported to summarize data that showed inferiority of African American intelligence relative to Whites. Others have reinterpreted their data, concluding that their findings may have been due to social policies (Fischer et al., 1996) or that their statistical analysis was flawed (e.g., Devlin, Fienberg, Resnick, & Roeder, 2002). An American Psychological Association (APA) task force (Neisser et al., 1996) concluded that "because ethnic differences in intelligence reflect complex patterns, no overall generalization about them is appropriate" (p. 96). The task force report itself generated much controversy (e.g., Ernhart & Hebben, 1997; Frumkin, 1997; Lynn, 1997; Melnick, 1997; Naglieri, 1997; Reed, 1997; Velden, 1997), with each author engaging in the debate arguing that others were influenced by their assumptions or biases. Our intent is not to revisit the controversy itself, but to point out first that researchers' worldviews shape the questions they ask and the research they conduct, and second that it is critical that researchers understand the cultural ramifications of our scholarship.

We argued in chapters 2 and 3 that it is critical that we as psychologists understand ourselves and other groups, also understanding that we may hold detrimental beliefs about others. We also need to be aware of potential beliefs we may hold that will influence our investigation. These assumptions affect the way we conceptualize a study, the variables that interest us, the location of the study, who is involved in helping shape the study, and the theoretical framework that shapes our research questions.

Consider Case Vignettes 1 and 2. Marlene is interested primarily in the effectiveness of a particular type of therapy, which may emerge from her own clinical practice. Julia's research question surfaces as a result of her work in her clinical practice as well, but it is inherently a question that involves the cultural differences in response to therapeutic modalities. Marlene appears to begin with an assumption that cultural differences will not affect her study and seems not to have incorporated race/ethnicity or gender differences that may have influenced treatment maintenance. Her research design may end up being compromised by the demographic differences in the treatment groups. Julia's research is framed by her assumptions that cultural differences affect preferences for treatment modality. However, although she appears to benefit from the perspective of the counseling center's director, she cannot assume that she is knowledgeable about the issues affecting ethnoracial minority clients. She should also engage in discussions with members of the various ethnoracial communities as she designs the specific research questions for her study.

RESEARCH GENERATION AND DESIGN

As we noted previously, the researcher's worldview frames the research question that is asked (Egharevba, 2001). It only makes sense that we psychologists investigate areas that are of interest to us or that are intriguing; often, this means our research questions are consistent with preferences for our own group. Heppner, Kivlighan, and Wampold (1999) pointed out that researchers' view of human nature helps to shape research questions, also noting that psychologists (indeed, all people) tend to pay attention to information that confirms already existing beliefs and do not attend to information that disconfirms our beliefs. This is particularly a problem when we believe that our worldview is universal and objective. Davis, Nakayama, and Martin (2000) referred to this as the *fallacy of objectivity*; they also referred to the *fallacy of homogeneity*, the assumption that all members of a group are similar. Fiske (1998) pointed out that this has long-term consequences, including lack of knowledge of how Whites are perceived by ethnoracial minority groups, because White researchers have been more interested in Whites' behavior. Ibrahim and Cameron (2005) leveled a fairly strong charge at White researchers, contending "much research is conducted to serve the self-interests of the researchers . . . [such as] to secure tenure or to support personal and/or common social prejudices" (p. 401).

As we argued in chapter 2, it is important for us as psychologists to engage in self-examination and multicultural growth, or such charges will continue to be made. In conducting psychological research, this can occur first as the research is being designed. Goodwin (1996) outlined this first part of the research process as including three distinct steps, noting that each is influenced by the cultural context of the investigator: generation of the research question, suitability of the research question, and then piloting the research question. Heppner et al. (1999) described three different types of research questions: descriptive, difference, and relationship questions. From a culture-centered perspective, descriptive research may include questions about what a particular group is like or questions about aspects of that group (e.g., career experiences of African American firefighters). Difference questions have been the most widely used type of research questions in cross-cultural work, most often to examine differences between Whites and ethnoracial minority individuals, or among ethnoracial minorities. Finally, culture-centered relationship questions are designed to investigate the relationship between two or more variables. Although researchers have studied relationships among variables for ethnoracial minorities, too often these have been essentially difference questions (e.g., How does the relationship between depression and anxiety differ for Whites and African Americans?).

Regardless of the type of research question chosen, it is also critical to base it on culturally appropriate theories and models (Quintana, Troyano, & Taylor, 2001). Heppner et al. (1999) noted that one of the first steps in starting a research study is to read widely, and we strongly encourage psychological researchers to read beyond the traditional psychological theories to be knowledgeable about—and if appropriate, to apply—indigenous theories when designing research studies. Thus, Julia, in Case Vignette 2, would be encouraged to read widely about types of cultural preferences for healing, beyond the traditional talk-therapies done by European American therapists with European American clients.

Goodwin's (1996) second step (suitability of the research question) includes consultation with members of cultural communities when conceptualizing research. It is particularly important to consider, and to take into explicit account, possible benefits of the research for the community (Fontes, 1998; Ibrahim & Cameron, 2005). Ibrahim and Cameron (2005) recommended involving members of the community as co-researchers from the beginning, providing services if so determined after data is collected, being sensitive to using research to empower communities, and providing full disclosure about risks involved in participating in research.

One of the criticisms of traditional psychological research is that it has been too focused on quantitative techniques designed to reduce variance among subjects, including variance due to race/ethnicity. Scholars have strongly encouraged psychological researchers to be conversant with many types of research tools, including quantitative and qualitative methods, understanding the strengths and limitations of each, and applying the appropriate design for the type of research question under inquiry (Atkinson, 1985; Costantino, Malgady, & Rogler, 1986, 1994; Highlen,

1994; LaFromboise & Foster, 1992; Marin & Marin, 1991; S. Sue, 1999; Suzuki, Prendes-Lintel, Wertlieb, & Stallings, 1999). Fisher et al. (2002) recommended that researchers have

> (a) an awareness of the importance of scientific, social, and political factors governing definitions of race, ethnicity, and culture; (b) an understanding of within-group differences; (c) familiarity with and skills in constructing and implementing culturally valid and language-appropriate assessment instruments; and (d) knowledge of the cultural and political circumstances of participants' lives. (p. 1024)

For example, psychologists need to be knowledgeable about how participants' worldviews and experiences influence their responses to surveys and questions (Clarke, 2000; Kim, Atkinson, & Umemoto, 2001; Westermeyer & Janca, 1997).

ASSESSMENT

The second area we will discuss under culture-centered research is assessment. Ibrahim and Cameron (2005) noted that criticism of traditional monocultural psychological research includes use of assessment tools that are culturally biased, at worst, and limited, at best. There is also an over-reliance on paper-and-pencil tests that may be inappropriate for use with some cultural populations. For example, the Hmong population is traditionally a cultural group that relies on verbal transmission of information, rather than on written transmission. Relying on paper-and-pencil tests with traditional Hmong participants may not provide researchers with adequate information. It is very important to know the populations on which assessment tools are normed and whether they are appropriate for individuals of different cultures. It is also important for psychologists to have a repertoire of techniques we can use to collect information (CNPAAEMI, 2000; Marin & Marin, 1991; Quintana et al., 2001; Spengler, 1998). It is also important for psychologists to assess the language competence of their clients (Acevedo, Reyes, Annett, & Lopez, 2003).

Marlene, for example, in Case Vignette 1, decided to use a standardized instrument. She should thus research whether it is appropriate to use with the different ethnoracial clients at the site, first assessing their language competence. She should also look into whether there are different norms available to interpret the data from the surveys. Julia, in Case Vignette 2, should think about the various ways she could collect information on the clients at the counseling center. She might, for example, conduct in-depth interviews with clients, as well as using a culturally valid and reliable instrument to assess whether different types of therapy have been equally effective in ameliorating symptoms of stress and depression. Most critically, psychologists must not use instruments that are not documented as adapted for their population of interest. This information should be in test manuals, as recommended by the APA "Ethical Principles of Psychologists and Code of Conduct" (APA, 2002; see also APA Web site version at http://www.apa.org/ethics). Paper-and-pencil tests also exclude people who are illiterate or may have limited reading abilities, regardless of their traditional methods of disseminating or interpreting information. People will not always explicitly state that they have difficulties with reading and writing; hence, paying close attention to their ability to use assessment tools that entail literacy skills is pertinent.

Language is often a concern for psychologists in using assessment tools, both for standardized surveys and interview techniques. If we psychologists are working with a population that is not conversant in English, can we translate the test into the new language? If this is done, it is critical to determine the cultural validity of our instruments (Samuda, 1998; S. Sue, 1999). First, we will want to know if the two tests are linguistically equivalent or if the test has been appropriately translated and the words are the same in the two tests (Azevedo, Drost, & Mullen, 2002). We will also want to know the conceptual and functional equivalence of the underlying constructs assessed in the two tests. For example, we will want to ask ourselves if the underlying constructs have the same meaning in the two cultures and whether the function of the behavior is the same across cultures. As an example of the latter, the English word *debate* on the Strong Interest Inventory (Harmon, Hansen, Borgen, & Hammer, 1994) was translated as *argument* in Spanish, yet the functions of each are different. Researchers are encouraged to be aware of those potential differences that may influence results.

Assessment of culture-bound disorders should also be carefully considered. For example, a Mexican woman who newly emigrated may seek help for *susto*, or "soul loss." Such feelings are often associated with "fright disorders" stemming from a stressful or traumatic event(s). Assessing such a feeling can be complicated. Often, psychopathological symptoms are connected to acculturative stress, which can be a long, pervasive process of adjustment for many immigrants and may not be interpreted through standard assessment tools (Dana, 1998). Thus, instruments often used in research, such as the Minnesota Multiphasic Personality Inventory—2 (MMPI–2; Butcher, Dahlstrom, Graham, Tellegen, & Kaemmer, 1989), would not necessarily be sensitive to cultural nuances such as susto.

ANALYSIS AND INTERPRETATION

The third area we discuss is a culture-centered approach to analysis and interpretation. Similar to our earlier discussion of the potential for biases in developing research questions, psychological researchers are encouraged to consider a variety of hypotheses that may explain their findings. This includes guarding against hypotheses that perpetuate "blaming the victim" in which ethnoracial minority differences are seen as individually determined instead of potentially as a result of living in a racist and oppressive society (Quintana et al., 2001). For example, in Case Vignette 1, Marlene cannot conclude that her treatment was effective for all populations because so many ethnoracial minority clients dropped out of treatment. She needs to consider that the treatment could possibly be biased against women or ethnoracial minorities as a hypothesis for her findings. The clients in her study may have also dropped out for some reason related to the therapy provided, the study itself, or some random factor. Concluding that treatment was effective for all populations would be in error if she did not examine (or at least acknowledge) that these alternative hypotheses helped to explain her findings.

A culture-centered approach to analysis and interpretation is also one of attending to the external validity of a study. In other words, to whom may the results be applied? S. Sue (1999) noted that too often in psychological research, psychologists attend (and are reinforced to attend) to issues of internal validity, such as the rigor of the study and how well the researchers have controlled for extraneous variables. Sue contended that we pay too much attention to internal validity at the expense of external validity, or the generalizability of the study. Is the sample diverse enough to be able to be generalized to large segments of the population? And G. C. N. Hall (2001) warned that in interpreting the results of a study, it is critical to identify those aspects of the culture that are unique to the group relative to other groups. If, for example, the study participants were Asian American college students, how would results be different for Asian Americans of a different age, generational status, geographic region, or country of origin? G. C. N. Hall (2001), S. Sue (1999), CNPAAEMI (2000), and Fisher et al. (2002) highly recommend that research teams include individuals from the cultural group under investigation.

Dissemination

One of the most recent set of concerns about culture-centered psychological research has to do with the dissemination of research findings, and more critically, with the importance that communities benefit from research conducted there. Exhibit 6.2 is reprinted from Ibrahim and Cameron (2005), outlining guidelines for research on ethnoracial minorities. Ibrahim and Cameron are particularly critical of researchers who want to conduct research in ethnoracial communities, enter into those communities as experts, collect data, and then leave without any concern about the effects of that research on the participants or about ben-

EXHIBIT 6.2

Guidelines for Future Research on Ethnoracial and Cultural Issues in Psychology, Counseling, and Psychotherapy

1. Know and understand the ignoble history of race and science, especially as it pertains to research.
2. Recognize the worldview of the community of color and its relevance to the researchers.
3. Obtain consent from the leaders and the people in the community and then determine on specific basis whether the consent was given.
4. Plan research projects conjointly by the community of color and the researchers.
5. Clearly define race and culture variables. Clearly describe the characteristics of the study and the comparison group and the current racial–cultural coding used.
6. Recognize that data on variables such as race, social class, culture, ethnicity, and gender can play a pivotal role in increasing awareness of inequities and stimulating changes in policies.
7. In publishing, recognize what information would violate the confidentiality of the community of color and the individuals within the community. To whom should the information be disseminated? How should the information gained be made accessible to the local communities?
8. Editors must play a major role in developing and implementing a policy on the conduct and reporting of research on race, culture and health.

Note. From "Racial–Cultural Ethical Issues in Research," by F. A. Ibrahim and S. C. Cameron. In R. T. Carter (Ed.), *Racial–Cultural Psychology and Counseling: Theory and Research* (Vol. 1, p. 408), Hoboken, NJ: Wiley. Copyright 2005 by Wiley. Reprinted with permission of John Wiley & Sons, Inc.

efits to the communities. Psychologists are encouraged to begin research studies with intent to benefit the participants' communities (CNPAAEMI, 2000; Ibrahim & Cameron, 2005; Marin & Marin, 1991). Specifically, Ibrahim and Cameron recommended that when researchers approach communities, they do so as psychologists with expertise to offer rather than as experts with the power to inform communities. They suggested that there must be direct benefit to communities, which may include technical assistance, psychological services, or helping with grant writing to support programs. Ibrahim and Cameron recommended that researchers work diligently to develop long-term relationships with partners in ethnoracial communities. They strongly urged psychologists to ensure that members understand enough about the project to give informed consent to participate. They further recommended that researchers work within communities to share data, rather than to assume that the researcher owns the data. These recommendations were developed to ensure that both the researcher and community leaders are accountable to conduct psychological research that is of benefit to ethnoracial minorities.

Typically, dissemination includes publishing a study in a journal or presenting the findings of the study at a conference. We recommend that psychological researchers report on participants' cultural, ethnic, and racial characteristics and also consider and report any limitations that may be due to cultural context. It is important to consider to whom the findings may be generalized.

Summary

As Lehman, Chiu, and Schaller (2004) noted, "Psychological processes influence culture. Culture influences psychological processes" (p. 703). It is hard to imagine a psychological variable that is not affected by culture; it is critical to explicitly incorporate culture as part of research. It also follows that all psychological research is shaped by the culture of the researcher and by the culture of the participants of a research project. This chapter presented an overview of the way that psychology has, or has not, incorporated culture in psychological research, and we have argued that is critical to do so at each point of the research process.

Psychologists as Organizational Change Agents

7

We are already deep in the new century, a century that is fundamentally different from the one we assume we live in. Things somehow don't fit.

—Peter Drucker

Guideline 6: Professionals are encouraged to use organizational change processes to support culturally informed organizational (policy) development and practices.[1]

Competency Statements

Psychologists committed to use organizational change processes to support culturally informed organizational (policy) development and practices will be able to articulate, enact, and give leadership to multicultural organizational change processes, empowered with knowledge about

- a Blueprint for Organizational Diversity (see Figure 7.1) and other models for multicultural organizational development that can be applied in different institutional settings,
- relevant terminology,
- specific methodologies and approaches to assess organizational change with particular sensitivity to multicultural diversity,
- examples of multicultural practices within organizations, and
- situations and settings wherein psychologists can be change agents and policy planners.

---

[1]Cited in "Guidelines on Multicultural Education, Training, Research, Practice, and Organizational Change for Psychologists," American Psychological Association (APA; 2003, p. 392; see also APA Web site version at http://www.apa.org/pi/multiculturalguidelines/).

Figure 7.1. Blueprint for Organizational Diversity.

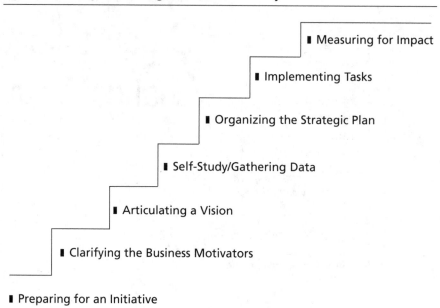

■ Measuring for Impact

■ Implementing Tasks

■ Organizing the Strategic Plan

■ Self-Study/Gathering Data

■ Articulating a Vision

■ Clarifying the Business Motivators

■ Preparing for an Initiative

Psychologists as Organizational Change Agents

In 2002, the American Psychological Association (APA) held a competencies-related conference to discuss "future directions in education and credentialing in professional psychology." One of the workgroups addressed consultation and interdisciplinary relationships and developed a schema for preparation in consultation competencies. The workgroup concluded that (a) consultation is a domain in professional psychology; (b) consultation is an interdependent process of context, competence, and implementation skills; (c) psychologists have many opportunities to be internal and external organizational change agents; and (d) multicultural guidelines and competencies must inform consultation processes (Arredondo, Shealy, Neale, & Winfrey, 2004). In many respects, Guideline 6 from the "Guidelines on Multicultural Education, Training, Research, Practice, and Organizational Change for Psychologists" (APA, 2003; see also APA Web site version at http://www.apa.org/pi/multiculturalguidelines/) captures these four conclusions and furthers the premise that psychologists grounded in consultation and organizational development preparation, informed by multicultural perspectives, can lead multicultural organizational development (MOD) initiatives.

This chapter is designed to be practical and to discuss hands-on approaches. Central to the chapter is the Blueprint for Organizational Diversity (Arredondo, 1996), applied in institutional settings to address workforce diversity. These settings range in size and include ad agencies, banks and other corporate entities, teaching hospitals, mental health centers, government agencies, colleges and universities, and multiple social service agencies. In all situations, it is evident that the skills sets of a psychologist, including assessment, evaluation, group work, research, and training, are highly valued and needed. Above all, however, interpersonal and collaborative skills are the most distinguishing factors among psychologists as change agents.

Additional features of this chapter are the case studies and an assortment of application tools. The Blueprint provides action steps and processes that involve the use of these tools for the implementation of a diversity initiative (DI). All of the materials have been used and proved useful in different organizations. Because a DI presumes change, psychologists may also consider the use of the Blueprint as a tool for other types of organizational change initiatives. These are adaptable.

In this chapter, we emphasize the preparation and assessment phases of the organization change plan. This occurs for several reasons. First, an ill-grounded DI easily leads to failure: Buy-in from multiple stakeholders, endorsement and engagement by senior leadership, clarity about the rationale for the initiative, and a clear communication strategy must be established in the preparation phase. Second, self-studies (with respect to diversity) need to be sensitively planned and positioned. Conducting a workplace opinion survey is very different than an organizational climate survey that focuses on diversity. Third, specific action strategies generally emanate from the self-study and the organization's strategic priorities, suggesting that this phase in an initiative is more client-centered and idiosyncratic. Similar findings from a self-study may likely apply similar and unique follow-up actions, because these are organization-dependent.

In the final section of this chapter, we provide examples of short- and long-term implementation strategies designed to contribute to institutional or permanent change. Some of our consulting work took place nearly 20 years ago, and we can now point to evidence of "institutional" change as a result of a continuous and deliberate focus on diversity and multiculturalism throughout these organizations.

Case Vignette 1: Midwest State University

The psychology faculty of Midwest State University was polarized. Graduate students had returned from APA's annual convention and organized a student diversity committee. The graduate student committee had existed for many years primarily for social events but was not active in departmental business. Faculty and students convened for the annual orientation session and collaborated at times for presentations at conferences. However, the department followed a traditional faculty–apprentice model. Student research was primarily based on faculty interests.

The student committee was a multiculturally diverse group, led by a White lesbian graduate student and a Puerto Rican man in his senior year. During their meetings over 2 months, the students developed a manifesto with 10 action strategies. The top 3 strategies were the following: (a) Students should have a seat at the faculty meetings to facilitate open dialogue on issues that affected students, in particular; (b) students and faculty should have a retreat to address multicultural diversity concerns; and (c) the faculty should endorse the APA Guidelines.

Faculty reaction to the student manifesto was visible shock, disbelief, and outrage. The faculty of 30 included 16 men and 14 women; 21 were tenured, including one Asian American man and a Latina. The only other person of color was an untenured African American woman, very popular with the students.

As chair of the program, how would you give leadership to this situation? How can the faculty be responsive to students while processing the manifesto? Of the top three manifesto items cited, which one of any should the faculty support? If you were invited to consult with the faculty, (a) how would you respond to their personal emotional reactions and (b) what strategies for professional responsiveness would you recommend?

Reflection on Case Vignette 1

Case Vignette 1 may become an increasing occurrence as students and faculty continue to recognize the empowerment provided by the institutionalization of the Guidelines. Similar scenarios are also playing out in college counseling centers, behavioral health agencies, and other workplaces that serve and employ diverse constituencies. Never before in the history of professional psychology has there been a convergence of divisions and psychology-related organizations motivated to work from multicultural perspectives, and never before in the history of the United States has there been such an increase in cultural diversity. The combination of these forces situates professional psychology on the precipice of organizational change in all areas—education and training, research, and practice.

Case Vignette 1 also illustrates the complexity of issues in a training program in which there may be significant incongruence in student–

faculty relationships because the senior faculty may not be current with contextual changes in the field and not sensitive to the students' previous requests. In Case Vignette 1, there are contemporary students who are sociopolitically aware. The students at Midwest State University are also the type of students who are active in professional graduate associations, are well-read, and are social justice advocates. This means they will make demands if the faculty brush them off too often. These are empowered and not passive individuals, and they are in psychology training programs, internship sites, and in postdoctoral settings all over the country. The endorsement of the Guidelines by the APA Board of Directors and Council of Representatives has become one of the most important internal and external motivators to pressure for change in the profession.

Planning for Multicultural Organizational Change

We now discuss the premises that ground multicultural organizational change and, if accepted, facilitate a smoother process for those leading and communicating about the change effort. These premises are embodied in the models for workforce DIs and other multicultural consultations in higher education and the private sector (Arredondo, 1996; Cox, 1993; Ibarra, 2001; D. W. Sue & Sue, 2003; Thomas, 1991, 1996).

Premises for multicultural organizational change include

- Multiculturalism is a fact of life: "It has always been and always will be" (Arredondo, 1996, p. 6).
- Organizations need to move from affirmative action to affirming diversity (Thomas, 1991).
- Multicultural diversity is a catalyst for organizational development and people must be the focus because "organizations and people are in interdependent relationships" (Arredondo, 1996, p. 11).
- The psychology of organizations is informed by economics, individual differences, human relations, and cognitive and social identity paradigms (Haslam, 2001); for MOD, these paradigms must be factored into the change and resistance to change dynamics.
- Organizations are systems, embedded in the society that surrounds them and therefore reflective of those national core values. In the United States, these values include individualism versus collectivism, competition, directness, and self-sufficiency, often becoming organizational norms for behavior.

- MOD requires a shift in thinking from structural functionality to visionary leadership that can empower and institutionalize the effects of the change process.
- Through deliberate multicultural organization planning, dignity and respect for individual and group differences and preferences can be honored.
- Institutions of higher education must become multicontextual if they are to retain and develop faculty, staff, and students of color and from underrepresented groups (Ibarra, 2001). According to Ibarra (2001), most universities are oriented to low-context behavior, accommodating primarily European American values for directness and highly verbal versus nonverbal behavior.

COMPETENCIES TO FACILITATE CHANGE

Planning and implementing organizational change processes is becoming a competency area for psychologists. As previously mentioned, one of APA's Competencies Conference workgroups focused on competencies for consultation and interprofessional collaboration. As a result of their collaboration, the workgroup outlined the different components of competency as (a) foundational knowledge about organizations, (b) cultural self-awareness, (c) specific skill sets, and (d) interpersonal skills (Arredondo et al., 2004). For psychologists to lead and influence multicultural organizational change, these competency areas are deemed essential. Guidelines 1 and 2 (see chapters 2 and 3) addressed the domain of cultural awareness specific to evaluating cultural identity and bias and its effects in cross-cultural interactions. These are cornerstone competencies for all psychologists.

The focus of this section is primarily on competencies related to knowledge building about MOD and DI as they tend to be called in many organizations. Psychologists as change agents need to be prepared in literature outside of psychology as much of the focus on organizational DIs has come from workforce diversity research and publications.

FOUNDATIONAL KNOWLEDGE ABOUT MULTICULTURAL ORGANIZATIONAL CHANGE

The publication of *Workforce 2000* (Johnston & Packer, 1987) precipitated attention to issues of workforce diversity primarily in the private sector. In response to the projected demographic changes discussed in chapter 1, employers focused on creating change by the recruitment, hiring, and advancement of women and persons of color and through the use of diversity training. Similar to the private sector, institutions of higher education responded to affirmative action policies through their student admissions and faculty- and staff-hiring processes. However, the strategies used were primarily designed to promote representation and individual self-awareness and were not oriented to systems of change. Organizational change or lack of change has been measured primarily through quantitative evidence of persistence or retention rates of underrepresented employees and students. These outcome data, however, are not direct indicators of multicultural organizational change processes because they are unidimensional. True change must occur at the "individual, organizational, and societal levels" (D. W. Sue et al., 1998, p. 6).

MODELS FOR MULTICULTURAL ORGANIZATIONAL DEVELOPMENT

Conceptual models for organizational change have been introduced to guide MOD. A continuum of cultural competency has been proposed to describe organizational and individual behavior (Cross, Barzon, Dennis, & Isaacs, 1989). This continuum describes organizations as demonstrating cultural destructiveness, cultural incapacity, cultural blindness, cultural pre-competence, cultural competence, and cultural proficiency. The most debilitating organizational behavior of cultural destructiveness embodies individuals' attitudes and the policies and practices they put in place that result in destruction of cultural identity. Examples include English-only policies in mental health centers that serve non–English-speaking clients or the use of IQ tests without norms for the groups being tested. Cultural proficiency, the positive end of the continuum, is characterized by organizational behavior that deliberately promotes the value of cultural pluralism. For example, in a university setting, faculty would teach graduate students how to conduct culturally responsive research on a Native American reservation. The cultural competence continuum can be used to assess the organization's status quo and to guide goals for change.

A cube model has been introduced by D. W. Sue et al. (1998) to conceptualize the different contexts and populations that require attention for MOD and training. The 3 × 3 × 3 matrix is recommended for assessing systemic and interpersonal barriers to desired goals for multicultural organizational change. In the model, three functional levels for assessment are proposed—recruitment, retention, and promotion. According to D. W. Sue et al. (1998), change can be facilitated through cultural diversity training that focuses on consciousness raising, sensitivity training, knowledge building about multiculturalism in the workplace, and cross-cultural management skills. These training foci directly relate to Guidelines 1 and 2, discussed in chapters 2 and 3. Guideline 1 addresses us psychologists as cultural beings, making it necessary for us to engage in awareness building about our worldview and experiences that bias, both positively and negatively, our beliefs about ourselves. Guideline 2 can be addressed through culture-specific education and sensitivity training. This guideline discusses psychologists' interpersonal, cross-cultural behavior with others. The cube model offers a graphic image about the complexity of organizations and their systems, processes, and people, with respect to promoting MOD in a broader rather than narrower context. With these contextual realities in mind, D. W. Sue et al. (1998) also recommended attention to the development of multicultural policies and leadership to strengthen the change process.

A third model to guide MOD or DIs is the previously introduced Blueprint, which is both systemic and developmental, outlining phases with specific goals and processes (see Figure 7.1). All phases and tasks are discussed in the next section. Essentially, each phase, beginning with preparation and planning and leading to implementation of change strategies, involves many meta-tasks and processes. Organizational change is not a quick process but is one that requires extensive collaborations, flexibility, adaptability, and patience. As discussed in *Successful Diversity Management Initiatives* (Arredondo, 1996), leadership is usually challenged because of the legitimacy of multicultural and diversity-oriented initiatives (Mio & Iwamasa, 2003), and it is essential to empower a committee with individuals who are respected within an organization.

To plan for and facilitate MOD, psychologists as change agents must recognize and communicate some of the criteria that reflect a multiculturally competent organization. The following checklist can be used in a variety of settings in which psychologists practice as change agents (e.g., teaching, clinical practice, research). The checklist in Exhibit 7.1 sets the stage to begin an initiative. Different settings are mentioned in the statements to bring attention to the practical application of this assessment tool that has been adapted for use with psychology departments, college counseling centers, behavioral health care organizations, hospitals, universities, not-for-profit organizations, and corporations.

Engaging in a Multicultural Organizational Development

TASKS FOR THE PREPARATION AND PLANNING PHASE

The preparation and planning phase in the Blueprint is the time to map out an organizational strategy, timeline, and resource allocation. As one

EXHIBIT 7.1

A Checklist for Planning DIs

This checklist requires "yes" or "no" responses.

- The institution has a mission and values statement reflecting multicultural diversity.
- There is a senior-level administrator or person designated to lead a multicultural organizational initiative.
- Senior administrators, directors, and faculty have educated themselves about the Guidelines.
- When it comes to excellence in multicultural diversity, other institutions would think of us.
- Our training program and counseling center has endorsed the Guidelines.
- For purposes of program planning, we have reviewed the demographic trends in our area for all constituencies, including persons of color.
- We provide special seminars, courses, and workshops regarding growing ethnic minority populations in our area.
- Our agency has developed promotional materials that may be attractive to ethnic minority populations.
- Our agency has developed bilingual intake forms and other documents that provide informed consent.
- We have an active referral list of ethnic minority agencies, health care providers, religious institutions, and other resources that can facilitate special client needs.

might expect, thoroughness in planning facilitates a smoother implementation of the organizational change process. It is recommended that the planning phase be allowed no less than 4 to 6 months. In this time, a few key tasks are recommended.

Establish a Multicultural Workgroup

The workgroup must be reflective of different constituencies in the organization. Those affiliated with a training program or counseling center should include students in the workgroup. Those affiliated with an agency should include nonclinical staff who are likely to interact with clients as well. Additionally, be clear about the authority of the workgroup and the reporting process. The size of the organization or department may determine this. If one is at a large behavioral health organization, the individual holding decision-making power may be the vice president of operations or the executive director. At a university, it may be the dean of the college or university provost.

Clarifying the Purpose and Functions of the Workgroup

The rationale and charge for the workgroup are generally articulated by an organizational leader with the authority to convene the group. This individual speaks on behalf of organizational leadership and must communicate openly about the purpose of establishing a multicultural initiative. A workgroup might be constituted because of retention issues of clinicians of color or because of a proclamation brought by students as in the case example. Although the issue may be narrow to begin with, as the process unfolds, other systemic issues will likely emerge. Thus, the convener of the workgroup must be clear about expectations.

One question to be asked is, "Is a plan of action or a particular strategy requested?" For example, in Case Vignette 1, among the 10 issues brought forth by the students at Midwest State University, 1 issue involves a seat at the faculty meetings. Because the students have taken their concerns to the dean as well, appointment of a workgroup may come from this level. To be responsive to the students and for public relations reasons, the dean may convene a college-wide workgroup, implying that the issues at hand are important for all students. However, the workgroup must be clear about their tenure. Normally a yearlong appointment of a workgroup allows for the organizational change process to begin and for the implementation of at least three to four of the phases in the Blueprint.

Group Process Considerations

Additional tasks in the planning phase include knowledge development and teambuilding. Typically, workgroups have limited expertise with organizational change processes and multicultural development models. Some of the references in this chapter may become resources to inform a workgroup. Another strategy is to reach out to a similar organization or department and to inquire about their experience with MOD. A third task is teambuilding, essential for a multicultural workgroup. Examples for interpersonal and cultural awareness skill building may be found in the discussion of Guidelines 1 and 2 in chapters 2 and 3.

Involving a Consultant

For institution-wide MODs, engagement of a consultant may be indicated. As has been previously mentioned, most psychologists have minimal experience facilitating MOD or group processes in the workplace unless they specialize in multicultural organizational consultation. The engagement of outside consultants can bring legitimacy to an initiative, provided these individuals are competent in facilitating change processes related to multiculturalism and diversity and provided they appreciate the context and business of the organization. When consultants take the lead, all members of the workgroup will have a greater opportunity for equitable participation.

Articulating a Vision Statement

Creating vision and mission statements specific to being a multicultural organization may be optional. It is not uncommon for a college or agency to have a mission statement and core values that affirm diversity and multiculturalism or indicate "respect for all individuals." If so, these statements may provide the necessary language to guide the MOD. Even the psychology department at Midwest State University, Case Vignette 1, may have a mission statement that reflects diversity. If it does not, however, this may become a task for the workgroup.

Case Vignette 2: The Center for Healthy Living

At a weekly staffing at her APA-accredited internship site, the Center for Healthy Living, Carmela reviewed the file of a new Latina client. On the basis of her intake, she attributed the client's symptoms of depression to the women's unresolved issues of loss and grief as a result of immigration. Carmela's supervisor and other clinicians disagreed with her assessment, stating that the client, Señora Ramos, had been in the United States more than 15 years and so most likely does not have issues relating to immigration. Furthermore, Carmela was told that she was likely overidentifying with the client, because she too was an immigrant. Based on the staffing, Señora Ramos was assigned to a White, monolingual English-speaking therapist.

Clarifying Motivating Factors

Another step in the MOD process is the clarification of motivators or a rationale for an initiative. Diversity consultants have referred to this as the "business case" for diversity (Thiederman, 1991; Thomas, 1996). In other words, a workgroup must clarify reasons why a focus on ethnic/racial concerns is important to the organization's mission and values. A straightforward clarification task is to identify both external and internal motivators (Arredondo, 1996). External motivators may include accreditation, funding, image and perception by potential students or employees, reputation, and of course, local community pressure. Some internal motivators are retention of employees and students from underrepresented groups, the need for cultural competency foci in training and practice, ethical practice, and student complaints. The example from Midwest State University in Case Vignette 1 introduces multiple internal motivators for the program.

Case Vignette 2, with Carmela, points to possible external motivators for change. If Carmela were to approach local Latino politicians and leaders, their pressure on the agency might prompt attention to her concerns about the malpractice of the agency. As an intern, she is in a vulnerable position. By contacting individuals who can make determinations about the funding that goes to the Center for Healthy Living, she removes herself from the firing line and those in power can exert their authority. Another external motivator is the image of the Center as a provider of services, an employer, and internship site. A little bad press through informal channels could damage the reputation of any organization. In all instances, the well-being of clients must be the foremost concern.

Building Knowledge by Assessing Needs

Behaving like a learning organization (Senge, 1990) suggests becoming knowledgeable about current and potential forces that may affect one's organization. For example, today, more than 50% of college students are women. Projections suggest that this trend will likely continue, and perhaps increase, between now and 2020 (National Center on Education Statistics, 2003). In California, Latinos are expected to be the majority population in every age group under 50 by the year 2010 (Judy & D'Amico, 1997).

Learning organization practices include scanning the environment to notice changes that are occurring or that will potentially occur because of demographic shifts, technology, globalization, and economics. Of course the question that must then be asked is, "How are these changes going to affect our organization?" In addition to the external scan, organizations must also engage in an organizational diversity self-study. For graduate programs, this may sound like the self-study for accreditation; however, it is more comprehensive. The self-study we are referring to is an organizational assessment that invites feedback from the workforce, students, and possibly consumers and follows its own plan of action.

A multicultural organizational self-study involves a series of steps: planning and design, data gathering, data analysis, report writing, clarification of findings, and recommendations for next steps (Arredondo, 1996). These steps are outlined next.

PLANNING AND DESIGN OF A SELF-STUDY

Similar to the commencement of the entire initiative, extra time must be spent by the task force for the planning and design of a self-study. Among the decision-making tasks are the following: purpose and scope of the study; methodology (e.g., qualitative and quantitative) to be used; sampling procedures and potential participants; areas of inquiry through the use of surveys, focus groups, and interviews; logistics for implementing the study (e.g., mailings, Web-based surveys, location of focus groups for access and confidentiality); and communication strategies to the workforce and consumers. A communication plan must be in force throughout the life of an initiative to help employees understand the purpose of the organizational DI and alert them to events that they become involved in, such as the self-study. Communication may occur through regular organizational channels such as a newsletter, Web site announcements, or electronic mailing list.

INVOLVING CONSULTANTS

In our experiences, organizations often rely on outside consultants to assist with the MOD. These individuals bring the required expertise as well as independent, non-employee status. For example, in a university setting, the Human Resources (HR) manager recommended that her department conduct the survey and focus groups of faculty and staff, a way to save money. The task force, comprising faculty, staff, and students, quickly protested. Confidentiality was their principal concern, as well as prior issues with the HR department. Although not indicated overtly, there were also status issues. Faculty expressed great confidence in the consultants, individuals holding doctoral level credentials and with prior experiences in university settings.

DATA-GATHERING INSTRUMENTS AND PROCESSES

In the planning and design phase, the task force determines the types of data gathering that will occur. Vehicles for data gathering include organizational climate and diversity surveys, focus groups and interviews, and cultural audits. The organizational climate and diversity survey has been designed to tap multiple areas and behaviors in an organization, to examine how these are experienced by different constituencies and their level of importance for same. Among the categories in the proposed survey are "participation, recognition, trust, diversity, communication," and so on. Respondents are invited to provide two types of responses: their degree of agreement to statements about "participation" and the level of importance of these statements to them personally. For example, respondents may be given a statement such as "In our department, employees are asked for input before decisions are made that involve them." Using a 4-point Likert scale, respondents indicate *strong agreement* (1) to *strong disagreement* (4). Additionally, also using a Likert scale, individuals rate the level of importance of the statement from *very important* (1) to *not important at all* (4). The Diversity subscale on the survey poses 14 statements, inclusive of different constituencies (e.g., women; people who are lesbian, gay, bisexual, or transsexual [LGBT]; Native Americans; persons with disabilities; men; senior administrators; see Exhibit 7.2). These items also elicit agreement and importance scores.

A second part of the survey addresses a respondent's perceptions of the experiences of different constituencies as employees in the organization or as consumers. On a scale of 1–4, respondents rate the experiences of "White men, persons with disabilities," and other groups in the workplace. This role-taking evaluation process provides valuable information that often correlates with findings from part one of the survey.

The final section of the survey is a demographic information form. As with the entire instrument, this section is customized to reflect the different department, roles or positions, and titles in the organization. In a mental health center, the titles of senior administrators, clinicians, behavioral technicians, office personnel, HR, and managers may apply. The titles and departments in a university or membership organization such as APA would of course be different.

Focus groups and interviews follow the survey implementation process. In our experiences, this is indicated because areas of concern that emerge from the survey findings can be explored through direct inquiry. In several university-based studies, we added sections related to student behavior and issues of discrimination and harassment (see Appendix B). Based on findings in one study that more than 50% of the female respondents had experienced some form of sexual harassment, the consultants were able to inquire about this in the focus groups and interviews. Because harassment may have different meanings, clarification of experiences was essential. In another study, alcohol abuse was rated as the most important problem area at the university by all respondents. This finding was important to senior administration, particularly the departments of student affairs and safety, and became a call to action.

To provide more open, yet confidential, discussion, it is recommended that focus groups be composed of individuals with a shared affinity (e.g.,

EXHIBIT 7.2

Workforce Diversity and Inclusion

	Agreement				Importance			
Q11a. There is open acceptance of all dimensions of human diversity (e.g., ethnicity, race, gender, age, disability, lifestyle, religion, sexual orientation, etc.) in the faculty, administration, and staff at the College.	1	2	3	4	1	2	3	4
Q11b. All faculty and administrative staff are respected and valued for who they are as well as for what they do at the College.	1	2	3	4	1	2	3	4
Q11c. Faculty, administrators, and staff of all racial/ethnic backgrounds are valued and respected equally at the College.	1	2	3	4	1	2	3	4
Q11d. Faculty, administrators, and staff are comfortable with other faculty, administrators, and staff whose race/ethnicity is different from their own.	1	2	3	4	1	2	3	4
Q11e. Faculty, administrators, and staff of different races and cultural backgrounds communicate openly and effectively with each other.	1	2	3	4	1	2	3	4
Q11f. Faculty, administrators, and staff of both genders are valued and respected equally at the College.	1	2	3	4	1	2	3	4
Q11g. Faculty, administrators, and staff of differing religions are valued and respected at the College.	1	2	3	4	1	2	3	4
Q11h. Faculty, administrators, and staff of all ages are valued and respected equally at the College.	1	2	3	4	1	2	3	4
Q11i. Faculty, administrators, and staff of differing sexual orientations are valued and respected equally at the College.	1	2	3	4	1	2	3	4
Q11j. People in leadership positions are comfortable with faculty, administrators, and staff whose race/ethnicity is different from their own.	1	2	3	4	1	2	3	4
Q11k. The College's stated commitment to workforce diversity and inclusion is reflected in College policies and practices.	1	2	3	4	1	2	3	4

Note. From the organizational climate survey developed by Patricia Arredondo and Richard Woy.

female support staff, clinicians of color). Most work settings continue to have an underrepresentation of persons of color in professional and administrative roles, and therefore, oversampling of these groups through focus groups and interviews is always indicated. Individuals best suited for interviews are the senior administrators and any other individuals who may request anonymity.

The cultural audit is an information tool that is generally completed by individuals who know the organization well (see Appendix B). It is recommended that a senior officer, such as the executive director, chief executive officer (CEO), or HR director complete the audit. In large organizations with multiple departments and with 25 or more employees, the audit has been completed by the department head. The audit provides quantitative baseline data regarding management or administration, staff, products and services, marketing and customer or client relations, organizational environment, and activities to promote effective organizational diversity.

DATA ANALYSIS

This discussion continues to presume that consultants are partnering with the task force and managing the organization's self-study. Survey data should always remain in the hands of the consultants. Returning hard copies of the survey to the consultant and having the consultant manage a Web site for a survey is essential. The creators of the survey have used the Statistical Package for Social Science (2005) to create the data files that lead to statistical analyses. To better understand feedback for more than 100 items, the data is analyzed in three principal ways: by gender, ethnicity/race, and job role or position. Thus, in addition to a global score for all participants on the entire survey and different sections of the survey, analysis by the three primary demographic variables occurs. The results are informative about the varying experiences of the organization's climate by different constituencies. Do women and men have the same type of workplace experience with respect to "trust, participation, and recognition"? Do students of color have the same type of university experience as do White students? Do junior and senior faculty men have the same type of workplace experience? The responses to these three questions are generally "no"; however, the crucial information lies with the degree of difference of experiences, the categories in which there are the greatest disparities, and the representativeness of these results for the entire organization. Are those with the least representation or with least power in the organization providing the lowest agreement scores? Are they least satisfied?

As had been previously indicated, the focus groups and interviews offer another opportunity to explore areas of concern that emerge on the survey. Sample questions may inquire about how, from the participants' perspectives, the organization under study compares with similar organizations, the benefits and shortcomings for individuals who work or study there, and recommendations for making the organization more multicultural in theory and practice. With the qualitative data, a thematic analysis is conducted to identify primary and secondary themes. Grounded theory principles and techniques (Strauss & Corbin, 1998) are recommended to guide the analyses. This approach allows for all of the data to be examined together and for the emergence of explanations, as well as new theories, about the climate for multicultural diversity in the organization.

The organizational cultural audit provides another level of analysis about organizational practices and behaviors, relevant contextual data. Findings through the use of the audit may provide direction for the administration's planning for organizational diversity. Items in the "Public Relations" section inquire about outreach to ethnic minority community groups and the use of marketing materials that reflect cultural diversity. If the organization is not engaged in either of these practices, these may become part of the organization's strategic plan for change. As an illustration, in a university setting, 12 department heads in a college of education completed the audit. A similar practice occurred in a hospital setting and a social service agency with multiple sites. The beauty of the cultural audit is in the identification of discrete areas or behaviors that are strengths or in need of attention for an entire organization or in particular departments or units.

In learning organization terminology, the use of multiple assessments provides *double-loop learning*, that is, the opportunity to "take a 'double-look' at the situation by questioning the relevance of operating norms" (Morgan, 1997, p. 87) or other practices as a result of findings from the self-study. In other words, if data from the survey and through focus group discussions point to concerns about disrespectful communication from supervisors, and the audit indicates that there is no supervisory training taking place, organizational norms for staff development will come into question. The combined data from these assessments will lend support to the need for an organizational response specifically to supervisory training and on a larger scale, to issues of interpersonal disrespect. The latter is a detriment to MOD.

The data analysis process requires considerable time and deliberation. It may be easy to dismiss or jump to conclusions about the reported "negative" experiences of persons with disabilities or other underrepresented groups in the workplace. These findings require more questioning by the task force with the consultants to find possible explanations. Questions may be, "Is this happening in a specific department or throughout the organization?" "How many individuals are in the sample and what percentage of the respondents is reflected in the responses?"

As another illustration, looking again at the illustration about Midwest State University, it is likely that the profile of responses from students and faculty in the psychology department would be at variance. Students would likely rate survey items about "participation" and "diversity" lower than would faculty. On the cultural audit, the department chair might find that responses are primarily "no," indicative of few to no behavioral practices that support MOD.

Findings must be reviewed relative to the purpose of the study and the organization's mission. The data analysis process is another double-loop learning opportunity. Data from self-studies typically provide information about the strengths, shortcomings, and areas in need of improvement. In their data analysis, skilled consultants will be able to highlight areas in dire need of attention that may have greater implications for institutional policies and legal mandates. For example, if the incidences of experienced and witnessed racial harassment are reported by more than 50% of the female respondents, this fact would require immediate attention.

CAUTIONS ABOUT SELF-STUDIES

Working as organizational consultants overseeing self-studies has informed the following cautions that are offered. First, self-studies raise expectations and anxieties. If administrators fail to follow through with the communication of findings and to provide responses to recommendations that emerge from respondents, the MDI will be called in to question or perceived as unimportant. Second, there is always greater risk for underrepresented individuals or groups in an organization. Considerable care must be exercised with reports from White and ethnic minority individuals. Because there typically are very small numbers of ethnic minorities or other minorities (e.g., LGBT), quantitative survey data are collapsed so that findings of all ethnic minorities are reported as one score. Third, defensiveness by senior administrators may occur, particularly with unfavorable findings. In these instances, it is the external consultant who must assume the responsibility to help to interpret the findings rather than the task force. Because the latter is a group of employees, they may be more cautious about trying to offer explanations to their employer. Fourth, findings from a self-study must give direction to the organization in pursuit of its multicultural diversity development process. Thus, the consultants can offer both short- and long-term recommendations for specific areas and practices in need of attention. The self-study is not an end point but rather a planning tool for change. (See Exhibit 7.3.)

EXHIBIT 7.3

Guidelines for the Assessment Process

- Have clarity about the motivators for the self-study.
- Determine who could best lead the self-study.
- Review the principles of learning organizations.
- Develop guiding questions—What do you want to learn?
- Develop a work plan for the study because of the multiple tasks involved.
- Be prepared to respond to resistance from multiple levels of the organization.
- Practice ethical and culturally responsive behavior throughout.
- Review the different steps outlined in this chapter; they are based on real life experiences.

COMMUNICATION OF FINDINGS

A final and essential task in the phase termed "building knowledge by assessing needs" is a communication plan. Timeliness, preparedness, openness, and clarity are factors to guide this process (Arredondo, 1996). There must be consideration of multiple means of communication (e.g., forums, Web site, newsletter) and the different constituencies who need to be included. Forums or town halls may be for the entire organization and may be repeated at multiple sites as well. Department heads may also be charged with reporting on the findings at their staff meetings. Of great importance to this communication plan are the presenters or "messengers" of the findings. They must have credibility. In *Communicating Change*, Larkin and Larkin (1994) reported that the most reliable messenger is usually the individual with the most direct supervisory relationship such as a department chair. Nevertheless, the presence of a CEO or individuals that authorized the study must be part of the formal reporting process.

The type of organization will also dictate the most legitimate presenters. In some instances, members of the task force in the presence of the CEO make the report. Our experience in university settings is that the consultants are viewed with credibility and expertise and thus are in the best position to report on the study they directed. When conducting studies in human service agencies, the board of directors is one of the constituencies who hear or receive a report of the findings.

ARTICULATING GOALS AND STRATEGIES

The results of a self-study can promote the MOD process through specific action planning and implementation. Action planning must be informed

EXHIBIT 7.4

Sample of Organizational Issues

Organizational culture issues or concerns	Interpersonal behavior issues or concerns	Systems issues or concerns
Failure of faculty to attend to issues of cultural diversity in training, research, and practice	Exclusion versus participation of students in program business	Need for adoption of policies that reflect state of the art in psychology (i.e., Guidelines)

by findings from the study, best practices outlined in the Guidelines, and other relevant research and practices for MOD for the specific setting (e.g., college counseling center).

A question that often emerges in the planning process is, Do we need a special strategic plan for multicultural development separate from the institutional or departmental strategic plan? There is more than one answer to this question. Because multicultural practices are fundamental to all organizations, this focus needs to be woven in to all business areas and strategic initiatives. For example, most institutions have a community relations department with specific measurable objectives. If findings from the study indicate that the community relations department has not made outreach to ethnic minority constituencies or other underrepresented constituencies, this may become a new objective and practice for the department. Another example can be offered from Case Vignette 2, about the Center for Healthy Living.

The experiences of Carmela, the psychology intern at the Center for Healthy Living, revealed practices that would likely emerge in a multicultural organizational assessment. These are that the organization has few to no resources to address Latino clients in need of services; clinicians are in need of multicultural competency workshops as well as ones specifically focused on working with Latinos; and organizational administration must anticipate staffing needs, both clinical and nonclinical, to address the different cultural and linguistic needs of clients. Identified issues and concerns for the Center for Healthy Living can become objectives for change. Here, again, the objectives fit into an organization's strategic plan because they benefit the whole.

A template that has been used for analysis and planning involves three domains: (a) organizational culture issues or concerns, (b) interpersonal behavior issues or concerns, and (c) systems issues or concerns (Arredondo, 1996). Feedback from the three assessment tools can be

EXHIBIT 7.5

The Report-Card Model

Issues	Measurable strategy
Sense of isolation among ethnic minorities	Research teams include ethnic minorities
In-group and out-group behavior	Peer and faculty mentoring arrangement
Faculty is not current on multicultural research	Faculty attend national conferences that specifically address multiculturalism in psychology and mental health
Recruitment and selection processes for new faculty	Consulting with other programs that seemingly have good representation of ethnic minority faculty and students (APA Suinn minority achievement awardees)

applied to all three areas. Exhibit 7.4 outlines these assessment tools applied to Midwest State University, from Case Vignette 1.

Another format is a report-card model. On one side of the ledger is a column with the statement of issues and on the other side is a column with recommendations for action. Exhibit 7.5 shows this report-card model.

Issues can be reframed as recommendations or objectives, thereby helping an organization to be more specific or deliberate with its plans. Specific strategies for systems change that have emerged in multiple studies include the following: mentoring of ethnic minorities and other underrepresented individuals, regardless of status or position; promoting cross-racial dialogue; reducing in-group and out-group behavior, using culture-specific recruitment and selection processes; and infusing of multicultural and diversity perspectives into decision making. The latter practice can take place at multiple levels in the organization. For example at Midwest State University, in Case Vignette 1, students can be consulted when decisions are about them.

IMPLEMENTING CHANGE

With the results from a self-study and strategic priorities, implementation is the next stage. In all cases, implementation depends on leadership and collaboration of key stakeholders, key administrators, and others. A few examples follow.

In a behavioral health organization, the senior administration team enacted six immediate priorities as the direct result of feedback that emerged from the survey, but more important, from the focus groups.

Anecdotes were shared that raised the level of concern about the personnel director and about the professional development needs of the staff in order to be more confident about their work. In the short term, the senior administration reassigned a personnel director who was gatekeeping applications of persons of color, instituted pay differentials for bilingual clinicians, purchased culture-specific artwork for waiting areas and office spaces, promoted a Latino senior manager to the position of vice president for diversity, appointed an African American professional to the Board of Directors, and established quarterly professional development seminars to address culturally competent clinical practice. A few of the agency's long-term goals were as follows: hire a minimum of two bilingual clinicians for their four sites, partner with a local university to develop a pipeline of future clinicians from a graduate program, and change personnel policies so that cultural competency could be part of performance reviews.

Other examples come from college counseling centers at large research universities. In these settings, there is an increasingly diverse student population, many of whom are first-generation; others who are coming out, claiming their LGBT identity; and some with typical developmental, adjustment issues. The self-study in these settings often revealed concerns by staff about their preparation to work with a "new" type of student. Change strategies to promote multicultural competence in college counseling centers focus on goals such as relationship development, staff education and training, and revision of the mission and value statement. To enact these goals, the counseling center staff reaches out and partners with student organizations as a way of building trust and showing support. To be responsive to staff, task forces are established to make recommendations for in-service training. This results in regularly scheduled multicultural competency training, support for staff to attend multicultural conferences, and responses to specific requests by individuals. In these counseling centers, evaluation of progress is a key practice. The evaluation is designed to assess progress toward goals as well as for new goal-setting.

Other Considerations in a Multicultural Organizational Transformation Process

All organizations are cultures grounded in a historical past that may or may not appear to be relevant in contemporary society. In some institutions of higher education, there are efforts to remove the tenure process, a heresy for many academics. As with any change initiative, there will likely be different forms of support and resistance to a multicultural organizational agenda. For this discussion, the enablers and barriers, usually "different sides of the same coin," are mentioned.

Enablers:

- clear definition of terms and purpose and rationale for the initiative;
- a blueprint for the process and timeline for the initiative;
- leadership from senior administrators;
- knowledge and credibility of the task force;
- credibility of the consultant(s);
- accurate, well-timed, and broad-based (i.e., to all constituencies) communication;
- the organizational culture, and more open systems with learning organization values and practices;
- shared accountability for the outcomes of the initiative beyond the task force and consultant;
- willingness to measure change 3 and 5 years later; and
- external and internal motivators for the initiative (e.g., demographic changes, competition, image).

Barriers:

- "unreasonable" expectations of the outcomes of the initiative in the short term (e.g., organizational culture will be more participatory immediately);
- confusion about affirmative action and a multicultural DI that is not mandated by law;
- human resistance, that is, unwillingness to be part of the change process;
- institutionalized racism, sexism, and other forms of discrimination;
- defensiveness and sense of threat because of proposed change; and
- consultants not prepared for work in a particular setting, that is, consultants who are content smart but not context savvy.

All organizations have a worldview that informs their beliefs, values, traditions, and other practices that make the organization what it is. To organizational leaders, these are sacred and often perceived as untouchable. For example, at Midwest State University, in Case Vignette 1, the idea of including students in faculty meetings may seem countercultural to some individuals because it is nt normative behavior in the psychology department. At the Center for Healthy Living, in Case Vignette 2, "listening" to, and taking counsel from, an intern may also be nontraditional behavior. This is not to suggest that behavioral change is impossible in these two settings but to indicate that differing perspectives, if not understood, could lead to unnecessary stalemates or conflicts. Most people believe they are fair-minded, inclusive, and not intentionally discriminating.

Leadership

MOD is a new way of thinking about organizational change, and how leaders understand this paradigm and their experiences with it are essential to the change process. In the preceding chapters, we discussed the Guidelines. The successful implementation of multicultural perspectives in education and training, research, and practice depends on well-informed psychologist leaders, administrators, and faculty. Students, interns, and nonadministrative staff will look to these program leaders for clues. For instance, regarding Case Vignette 1, if it appears that the faculty of Midwest State University is opposed to endorsing the Guidelines, the gap of trust between faculty and students will likely widen. Regarding Case Vignette 2, the agency director at the Center for Healthy Living has the opportunity to assert leadership with Carmela and her supervisor. Because of Carmela's bilingual and bicultural capacity, she would possibly better serve the new client than a White, non–Spanish-speaking therapist. By intervening and making the change, the director would model respect for the value of cultural and linguistic responsiveness versus cultural malpractice.

The Future of Multicultural Organizational Development

Multiculturalism is a fact of life (Arredondo, 1996) and is in the fabric of many institutions, from the media to the corporate world. Because multiculturalism is about people, the human dimensions of society, there is every opportunity for psychologists to be leaders in institutional agendas for multicultural diversity. Through APA, there has been leadership at federal levels for policy changes regarding important social issues (e.g., reparations and the U.N. World Congress Against Racism in 2003) and underrepresented groups (e.g., same-sex marriages). From APA, there are important documents that inform education and training, as well as research and practice, with underrepresented groups. These documents on research and practice with ethnic-specific groups (APA, 1990; Council of National Psychological Associations for the Advancement of Ethnic

Minority Interests, 2000, 2003), from gerontological perspectives, and with clients who are LGBT (APA, 2000) complement the APA "Ethical Principles of Psychologists and Code of Conduct" (APA, 2002; see also APA Web site version at http://www.apa.org/ethics/) and cultural considerations indicated in the latest revision.

Multicultural organizational change is a developmental process. For individual psychologists, implementing the Guidelines provides new ways of thinking and enacting psychology. All of us as psychologists will have new learning curves in this regard. Becoming knowledgeable through the literature and engaging in learning opportunities through multicultural-focused conferences, such as the National Multicultural Summit, and other collaborations with ethnic minority community associations will only strengthen our shared capacity to lead MOD. In the words of a civil rights and social justice advocate, the late César Chávez, *sí se puede*—Yes, we can.

Summary

Since the passage of the Civil Rights Act in 1964 and the enactment of Affirmative Action and Equal Employment Opportunity policies, employers, government agencies, and universities have been charged with applying these policies of inclusion. The most typical response has been to focus on the recruitment and hiring of underrepresented individuals, particularly women and persons of color. However, bringing in the outsider without changing internal structures and systems and the climate of the organization has perpetuated the status quo in institutions and even APA.

In this chapter, we outlined the Blueprint to plan and implement organizational change processes to support culturally informed organizational (policy) development and practices. Our premise is that a deliberate plan for MOD that addresses issues of access, shared power, and visible representation is necessary to promote individual, institutional, and societal well-being. Specific methodologies and approaches to assess organizational change with particular sensitivity to multicultural diversity have been provided.

Concluding Thoughts: Psychology as a Transformed Profession

8

Can you lead your people without seeking to control?
Can you open and close the gates in harmony with nature?
Can you be understanding without trying to be wise?
Can you create without possessiveness, accomplish without taking
credit, lead without ego? This is the highest power.

—Tao, 10

Competency Statements

Psychologists committed to multicultural centered practices will be able to demonstrate

- recognition of competencies and resources to enhance education and training, research, practice, and multicultural organizational change strategies, congruent with ethical behavior;
- recognition of barriers and enablers within the profession and institutions to promote culture-centered psychology;
- knowledge and abilities to address different forms of resistance to culture-centered practices; and
- knowledge about future directions for psychology through an integrated culture-general, culture-specific, and multidimensional contextual lens.

Overview

We have argued throughout this book that traditional psychology has had too much reliance on Western, European, White male perspectives and assumptions and has acted as if those assumptions and perspectives

EXHIBIT 8.1

Examples of Resistance to Culture-Centered Practices

How would you respond to these typical types of resistance to culture-centered practices?

1. Good counseling is good counseling. Everyone is the same, and we don't need special treatments for some.
2. There aren't good multicultural standards for sound practice.
3. Cross-cultural counseling competencies are too vague to be useful.
4. The multicultural practices suggested here are too complex to train students.
5. We don't have enough outcome data to know if multicultural competencies are effective.
6. These guidelines are not inclusive enough of other forms of diversity.
7. This is reverse discrimination and racism, and does not acknowledge the many contributions of European American psychology.

are universal. We contend that this traditional and culturally encapsulated paradigm in psychology has had a detrimental effect on the clients, students, research participants, and communities of color on whom those Western values and perspectives have been imposed. We hope we have also demonstrated how we psychologists can be more effective as teachers, practitioners, researchers, and change agents as we increase our knowledge and skills in culture-centered practices. Although we have discussed the need for culture-centered practices in the here and now throughout this book, in this chapter we present our perspectives about the potential for the future of psychology as a culture-centered profession. This chapter projects our vision for additional areas of growth for the profession as a whole, as well as our vision for specific steps we can take as psychologists and as an association of psychologists.

Before we talk about our vision for the future, we address the typical sorts of resistance that the psychological profession has had to overcome in becoming more culture-centered. Consider the types of resistance identified in Exhibit 8.1. D. W. Sue et al. (1998) called these the "seven deadly resistances" (p. 28).

Our discussion in chapter 2 can help lead readers through responses for some of the areas of resistance. The first resistance may also be called the "color-blind" resistance, in which individuals believe that minimizing differences between groups promotes greater equality. However, according to M. B. Brewer and Brown's (1998) review of the research on effectiveness of color-blind approaches, "ignoring group differences often means that, by default, existing intergroup inequalities are perpetuated" (p. 583). In other words, by not acknowledging differences due to culture and the need for culturally specific interventions, psychologists create unequal treatments. We also noted in chapter 4 that the U.S. Surgeon General's report, *Mental Health: Culture, Race, and Ethnicity* (U.S. Department of Health and Human Services [USDHHS], 2001) documented that, in fact, counseling is not the same for all and that effective treatment needs to be tailored to meet the needs of ethnoracial clients.

D. W. Sue et al. (1998) suggested that ethnocentric multiculturalism underlies most of these resistances; we add an additional reason based on categorization theory. As we noted in chapter 2, all individuals like to believe that their own group is positively valued and tend to then devalue other groups. Self-categorization theory may underlie a resistance that culture-centered practices preclude an appreciation of European American contributions to psychology. We certainly have not intended to convey such an attitude, rather to remind us that it is but one perspective, and to also note the damage that can be done if we assume the European American, Western perspective is the only view of psychology. A common value in that European American perspective is a high level of importance on the scientific method and on linear specificity (Katz, 1985). This value may underlie the resistances listed in Points 2 and 5 in Exhibit 8.1. Indeed, we agree that more research is needed on various forms of treatment; we discuss this more fully later in the chapter. However, we already know that our current practices are not as effective as they could be, so waiting for many levels of empirical support to change our practices seems to us to be less than ethical. As we noted in chapter 1, the American Psychological Association's (APA's) "Ethical Principles of Psychologists and Code of Conduct" (APA, 2002; see also APA Web site version at http://www.apa.org/ethics/) enjoins us as psychologists to do no harm and to respect the dignity of all.

We have encountered the resistance in Point 6 in Exhibit 8.1 a number of times as our writing team sought feedback on the Guidelines. In many ways, we agree that we have had a very narrow focus on diversity in this book, and indeed, we point out throughout the book that individuals have multiple identities and contexts in which they live. The personal dimensions of identity model (Arredondo & Glauner, 1992), which we discussed in chapter 2, in fact, notes that the A Dimensions of identity are shaped by gender, sexual orientation, social class, and physical ability, as well as by race and ethnicity. All of these are critical aspects of an individual's identity and may interact with each other. For example, a Mexican American lesbian may not find it important to differentiate the dimensions of her identity shaped by her ethnicity, sexual orientation, or gender. For her, it is just as important that we, as practitioners, understand that all of these may influence her behavior. Thus, we believe that as psychologists we need to be knowledgeable about all aspects of behavior; however, we also believe that focusing rather narrowly on the interactions specific to race and ethnicity helps us to increase our competence in this area.

Although the resistances listed in Exhibit 8.1 may stem from unconscious ethnocentrism ("my cultural way is the best way") and preferences for one's own group, they may also come from a fundamental resistance to changing the way one has always done things. We know as psychologists that pushing people to change, be they students, clients, or organizations, is hard. People resist change and continue in their comfortable patterns of behavior, even if they know those patterns are not the most functional. In addition, Arredondo (1996) found that defense mechanisms based on "fears, anxiety, or other unresolved emotions" (p. 213) serve as forms of resistance. Statements of denial often are that there is no problem in the organization and that everyone gets along. Blame is often used when changes are introduced by women or persons of color. Although these changes may be sanctioned by senior management, the underrepresented persons of color often become scapegoats.

We have argued explicitly in this book that the psychology profession needs to change. We have talked about changes needed in the way that we psychologists see ourselves and others and in the way we do our work as change agents, teachers, researchers, and practitioners. But more change is needed to transform the profession into a truly culture-centered field. We need to develop a deeper knowledge and awareness of the role of race and ethnicity in human behavior and of how we can provide leadership for effective culture-centered practices. Further, we need to look within professional associations such as APA that have established a wealth of resources to improve our work as culture-centered professional psychologists. The APA Office of Ethnic Minority Affairs (OEMA) is one destination point for these materials.

Future Directions

The theme of this book is change, systematic change by psychologists in a world that is culturally dynamic and increasingly pluralistic. Each of the six guidelines suggests that psychologists can assume leadership for our own continuous personal and professional development. Today, nearly 25 years since the Division 17 (Society of Counseling Psychology) task force issued "Multicultural Counseling Competencies" (D. W. Sue et al., 1982), there have been studies, literature reviews, and extensive theorizing leading to new models and concepts to advance understanding about the essentialness of culture to psychology. During this journey, multicultural advocates have created pathways throughout APA to bring resources to psychologists, pipelines of access to underrepresented groups such as ethnoracial minorities, scientific endeavors that strengthen the role of culture-general and culture-specific perspectives, and benefits for individuals we teach, involve in research, and work with in clinical situations. Additionally, through the leadership of the OEMA and the APA Public Interest Directorate, many of the issues that affect marginalized groups are addressed through advocacy for new federal policies. The application of the multicultural guidelines will continue to require steadfast APA governance leadership.

Opportunities for culture-centered change for individuals, professionals, and institutions have been discussed, and in many communities and institutions, there are efforts under way to bring cultural competencies in to practice. For example, the Arizona Council of Human Service Providers (2004) recently adopted a document for statewide culturally competent care: *Achieving a Culturally Competent and Linguistically Appropriate Human Service Delivery System* was prepared by their Diversity Committee and outlines an action plan for changing human service systems. They identified nine components for modifying their current system: communication, governance, organizational infrastructure, organizational values, planning, monitoring and evaluation, policy, practice, and workforce development. This collaborative endeavor is indicative of proactiveness in the midst of a sea of demographic growth, particularly for the Latino immigrant population in Arizona. Psychologists, social workers, counselors, and other change agents for private and public agencies joined forces because they recognized that managing and leading change for cultural competency must be deliberate. Because multiculturalism and diversity are facts of life (Arredondo, 1996), the time is now to engage in planning for, and responding to, culture-driven change.

Blueprint for Change in Organizations

In chapter 7, Blueprint for Organizational Diversity (Arredondo, 1996) was discussed, along with a sample audit for beginning an internal workforce analysis. We argued that representation of ethnoracial minorities is but one indicator of progress in heretofore primarily White institutions, including APA. In chapters 2 and 3, we identified dynamics, both conscious and unconscious, that contribute to the continued marginalization of underrepresented individuals and groups. In addition to counting heads, we discussed the importance of assessing for inclusive, welcoming, and supportive organizational climates. Representation, climate, and accountability for change are three of the main criteria that need to be applied in all organizations. It is possible to borrow from the Arizona Council of Human Service Providers' (2004) eight components as guideposts for change within APA governance, divisions, and staff; state and provincial associations; and the vast sea of institutions and organizations where psychologists teach, conduct research, and apply clinical skills.

As all organizations plan for change, there are demographic facts that can inform this process. The following data indicate the necessity to consider multiple identities as planning endeavors unfold. Clearly, all people are multidimensional, multicultural beings.

- Women outnumber men in the United States. As of 2000, the United States had 143 million women and 138 million men (U.S. Census Bureau, 2004).
- The percentage of women in the labor force in 2000 was 58.3%, as compared with 57.6% in 1990 and 50.5% in 1980. It has nearly doubled since 1950, when it was 30.2% (U.S. Census Bureau, 2004).
- With over 40 million Latinos in the United States, they are over 14% of the U.S. population. From 2000 to 2002, Latinos accounted for 3.5 million, or fully one half, of the population increase of 6.9 million (U.S. Census Bureau, 2004).
- Immigration and birth, particularly for persons of Latino and Asian heritage, account for percentage and numerical increases in the ethnoracial minority population.
- By 2005, Latino youth will account for 17% of those under 18; by 2010, 1 of 5 of all youths will be Latino. Among Latinos, persons of Mexican origin had the highest proportion under age 18—20% (U.S. Census Bureau, 2004).
- By 2008, ethnoracial minority groups will compose 29% of the labor force.
- By 2025, ethnoracial minorities, led by Latinos at 19.4%, will represent 40% of the total U.S. population.
- Islam is the fastest growing religion in the United States, with over 6 million Muslims.
- There are 1,209 mosques in the United States, with more than half founded within the last 20 years. This is the result of conversions to Islam.
- The largest segment of the American Muslim population is African American (Hedayat-Diba, 2000).
- American Indians represent approximately 2% of the U.S. population and are the largest ethnoracial minority group in Montana, the Dakotas, Idaho, and Wyoming.
- There are over 500 federally recognized, and close to 200 non–federally recognized, American Indian tribes.

- There is considerable diversity among the more than 550 American Indian tribes, making it impossible to specify that all individuals and tribes subscribe to similar values. Nevertheless, negative stereotypes held by well-intentioned researchers and clinicians continue to create cultural divides (Garwick & Auger, 2000; Herring, 1997).
- Persons of African descent were 12.3% of the U.S. population in 2000, with 16% of the increase since 1980 attributed to immigration (D. W. Sue & Sue, 2003).
- The heterogeneity of the population of African descent cannot be underestimated as immigrants from the Caribbean and Africa have had a different life experience than individuals with long-term roots in the United States, with its historical system of slavery.
- The Asian population in the United States continues to increase fueled by immigration from Southeast Asia (U.S. Census Bureau, 2004).
- The Asian population of 10,242,988 in 2000 was approximately 2% of the overall population (U.S. Census Bureau, 2004).
- Individuals who self-identify as Asian may be from Filipino, Chinese, Korean, and Japanese ethnic groups. Additionally, there are Southeast Asians from Cambodia, Vietnam, and Laos. The subgroups of Asian Indians from India and Pakistan contribute to the heterogeneity, principally foreign born (D. W. Sue & Sue, 2003).
- Pacific Islanders are also part of the Asian American history. Individuals from Guam, Samoa, and Hawaii introduce multicultural and multiracial diversity.
- Multiracial individuals were invited to self-identify as such in the 2000 U.S. Census, for the first time. Among those who self-reported, 93% indicated membership in two racial categories. The largest percentage (32%) marked White and another race. It is reported that the most common interracial marriages are among Asians and White Americans (D. W. Sue & Sue, 2003).

Summary

These are a few of the data with implications for psychological education, research, and practice. They challenge all of us, as psychologists, to reevaluate how we historically enacted our discipline. With such cultural heterogeneity as a reality, culture-specific and interdisciplinary approaches will become more necessary. We need to think about individuals as multidimensional, multicultural beings, coming from an array of contexts and having experiences that are, correspondingly, multicontextual. Be-

EXHIBIT 8.2

Putting the Guidelines to Work

- Develop your own developmental plan for becoming more culturally competent and hold yourself accountable. Evaluate yourself every 6 months—what have you learned about yourself and others and what do you aspire to learn?
- Think of yourself and others as multidimensional, multicultural beings who are also multicontextual.
- Identify ways that you can become more knowledgeable about and involved in communities of color. Determine ways you can form collaborations to make a difference.
- Identify ways that the systems in which you operate (your practice, your institution, your organization) create barriers or facilitators to culture-centered change. How can you be a facilitator for change?
- Inventory yourself. Create ways for people to talk about conflict with your peers and colleagues. Analyze unwritten rules and institutional messages in your organization. How do you benefit? Who does not benefit? Do you view the focus on diversity as an "add-on" or as integral to your work?
- As you conduct research, ask yourself how inclusionary and inclusive your planning process is. Using multiple methodologies and benefiting local ethnoracial minority communities has been advocated; are you following these guidelines?

coming more multiculturally oriented means engaging in more complexity while also appreciating individual differences. This complexity also means that we psychologists will have to step into more zones of discomfort, deal with our cultural and emotional dissonance, and still be culturally responsive.

Multicultural psychology serves as the fulcrum for interdisciplinary knowledge building, drawing on anthropology, history, medicine, economics, political data, and sociology to understand the human condition. Social psychology and social learning theories, in particular, as referenced in chapters 2 and 3, remind us of the roles of modeling, socialization, and other forms of learned behavior in various contexts, from the family, to the school, to the workplace, to governmental bodies. Multicultural psychology is rich and instructive about the interaction of people and their environments and about the role of history in the evolution of groups in a technological, global, and increasingly interdependent world. Rather than retreating to our specialties, we psychologists will have to collaborate with one another to make certain that trends such as positive psychology are inclusive of all groups.

Each ethnoracial minority group in the United States is highly heterogeneous, regionally distributed, and variable on many dimensions of personal identity. Although we may seem to be advocating for culture-specific awareness, knowledge, and skill development, we do not mean to suggest that psychologists rely on stereotypical descriptors. Throughout the book, we have recommended that psychologists consider context as well as historical and economic forces as an approach to understanding the worldview of the other. In so doing, we psychologists can all be change agents, eliminating barriers and making psychology a household word, a goal recognized by Ron Levant's term as president of the American Psychological Association in 2005. In Exhibit 8.2, we offer the recommendations to make psychology a multidisciplinary field of access, inclusion, and respect and dignity for all.

Closing Thoughts

Social justice advocates remind us of the obligation and responsibility all people have to one another. As professional psychologists, we believe this responsibility is even greater. In closing, we borrow from the words of civil rights leader César Chávez, whose example is worthy of our emulation: "Justice advocates remind us of the obligation and responsibility all people have to one another." As professional psychologists, we believe this responsibility is even greater. "We cannot seek achievement for ourselves and forget about progress and prosperity for our community . . . Our ambitions must be broad enough to include the aspirations and needs of others, for their sakes and for our own."

Appendix

Checklist for Culturally Competent Practice

A

1. Make a lifelong commitment to maintaining cultural expertise:
   a. Develop an awareness of personal preferences, biases, and cultural values that might impede effective delivery of services.
   b. Learn about cultural groups and variations that may relate to practice.
   c. Discover helping practices used in cultures other than the North American and European context that may be appropriately included as part of psychological practice.
2. Continually develop an awareness of issues of discrimination and oppression (e.g., racism, sexism, homophobia, classism) that clients might experience and develop an understanding of how these issues relate to presenting psychological concerns. Understand that many concerns stemming from oppression are not internal to the client but are externally part of the system in which he or she lives. In addition, psychologists are urged to find ways to address and dismantle oppression as part of their responsibility as competent professionals.
3. Pay special attention to the unique worldview and cultural background of clients. Be aware of how worldview and cultural background(s) interact with individual, family, or group concerns.
4. Recognize the client in context and view clients from a culture-centered perspective.
5. Be aware that contextual therapy may often require nontraditional interventions and recognize that special attention must be paid to ethical issues, such as confidentiality and boundaries.

     a. Recognize that even words such as *ethical*, *confidentiality*, and *boundaries* have varying interpretations, depending on world-view and context of therapists' practice.

     b. Understand "power" as defined within a cultural context.

     c. Become involved in a local community to understand its context. Activities may include serving on a local school board, attending festivals, reading local newspapers, or participating in a variety of cultural events.

     d. Seek out community leaders and influencers (spritual leader, healers, helpers) when appropriate, enlisting their assistance with clients as part of a total community healing approach.

6. Use culturally appropriate assessment tools and practices.

7. Examine traditional practice interventions for cultural appropriateness and contextual awareness.

     a. Seek to expand and interpret interventions, including multicultural awareness, action, and advocacy.

     b. Learn and apply new theories, concepts, and strategies from other cultures to enrich practice.

     c. Receive ongoing feedback and assessment on personal cultural competence. This may include peer review, client evaluation, and working on a culturally diverse consultation team.

8. Develop empirical research programs to evaluate, support, and clarify the effectiveness of what will be seen as "new" paradigms of practice.

     a. Use research to inform practice.

     b. Involve client communities in the development and interpretation of research.

     c. Engage in the dissemination of research results that clarify and add meaning to the uniqueness of clients.

     d. Challenge colleagues, organizations, continuing education providers, and professional training institutions to use these data.

Appendix

The Empowerment Workshops' Workforce Diversity Audit: An Organizational Self-Assessment

B

Purpose and Rationale

The purpose of this survey is to provide a profile reflecting the status of workforce diversity and cultural competency practices in your organization or work group. Questions in the audit are not designed to measure employee attitudes, values, or opinions. Rather, the audit is intended to determine to what extent your organization has carried out a variety of easily measurable actions that we have found to be associated with success in workforce diversity and cultural competency goals. The profiles resulting from completed audits can be used as benchmarks to measure your organization's progress in workforce diversity and cultural competency practices over time and/or as a way of assessing your organization's status in relation to other organizations of comparable size, type, or industry. The questions in the audit are grounded in over 15 years of research and professional experience at Empowerment Workshops, and the audit and resulting profile are closely integrated with our overall approach and our various specific services to help organizations achieve successful workforce diversity and organizational cultural competency.

Definition of Workforce Diversity

In the United States, workforce diversity refers primarily to cultural (linguistic) and racial diversity, including Asians, Pacific Islanders, and Alas-

---

Note: Used with permission from Patricia Arredondo and Richard Woy.

kan Natives, African American/Black, Hispanic/Latino, and Native American people working with mainstream White/Caucasian workers and with each other. In completing the audit, please use this definition of diversity as your reference point.

Who Should Fill Out the Audit

To assure accuracy and completeness, the audit should be completed by the head of Human Resources or another senior manager who has direct knowledge and ready access to the various activities, data, documents, systems, and procedures referred to in the audit.

What to Do Now

Please answer the questions on the following pages completely.

I. Management/Administration

1. Does the mission statement and/or strategic plan of your organization address issues of cultural/ethnic/linguistic diversity?
   Yes   No

2. Does the mission statement and/or strategic plan of your organization address issues of socioeconomic diversity?
   Yes   No

3. Are special efforts made to recruit, screen, and appoint senior managers who are from culturally and racially diverse backgrounds?
   Yes   No

4. What percentage of senior managers in your company are members of cultural/racial minority groups?
   0%–5%   6%–10%   11%–15%   16%–20%   More than 20%

5. Does the current level of diversity of senior managers represent an increase, a decrease, or no change in diversity compared to the past two years?
   Increased diversity
   Decreased diversity
   No change

6. Does the current senior management/administration group reflect the racial and cultural groups to whom the organization is trying to deliver services?
   Yes   No

7. During the past year, has the CEO/Executive Director or other senior manager addressed the issue of cultural/racial/linguistic/socioeconomic diversity in any speech, written statement, or other organization-wide or public way?

    Yes   No

8. Within the past year, have senior managers received training or consultation regarding issues of cultural/racial diversity?

    Yes   No

9. Please check whether each of the following reports/documents in your organization currently addresses and promotes cultural/racial/linguistic diversity. (For each item, check NA/Not Applicable only if your company does not currently have a specific report or document):

    Yes   No   NA   Annual report
    Yes   No   NA   Personnel policies
    Yes   No   NA   Job descriptions and qualifications
    Yes   No   NA   Strategic plan
    Yes   No   NA   Performance evaluation/incentive guidelines
    Yes   No   NA   New employee orientation materials and procedures
    Yes   No   NA   Brochures and marketing materials
    Yes   No   NA   Operating policies and procedures
    Yes   No   NA   Mission statement
    Yes   No   NA   Other (Specify): _____

10. Do current performance evaluations and incentives for senior managers tend to promote, limit, or fail to address performance in the area of workforce diversity?

    Promote diversity
    Limit diversity
    Do not address diversity

II. Staff

11. Are formal proactive efforts made to recruit, screen, and hire a workforce that represents the cultural, racial, and linguistic clientele being served?

    Yes   No

12. Are formal proactive efforts made to develop, promote, and retain employees who represent the cultural, racial, and linguistic clientele being served?

    Yes   No

13. What percentage of middle managers/supervisors in your organization are members of cultural/racial minority groups? (Check NA if your organization is too small to have a middle management group.)
0%–5% 6%–10% 11%–15% 16%–20% More than 20% NA

14. What percentage of clinicians are members of cultural/racial minority groups?
0%–5% 6%–10% 11%–15% 16%–20% More than 20% NA

15. What percentage of direct service providers (not clinicians) are members of cultural/racial minority groups?
0%–5% 6%–10% 11%–15% 16%–20% More than 20% NA

16. What percentage of support/clerical staff are members of cultural/racial minority groups?
0%–5% 6%–10% 11%–15% 16%–20% More than 20% NA

17. What percentage of maintenance staff are members of cultural/racial minority groups?
0%–5% 6%–10% 11%–15% 16%–20% More than 20% NA

18. Does the current level of diversity of the workforce represent an increase, a decrease, or no change in diversity compared to the past 2 years?
Increased diversity
Decreased diversity
No change

19. Specify the groups for which there has been a:
❑ percentage and numerical increase: _____
_____
❑ percentage and numerical decrease: _____
_____
❑ no change _____
_____

20. Are employees of color currently "clustered" in specific roles or job categories by race and ethnicity rather than being distributed throughout the workforce in a variety of job categories and levels?
Yes   No

21. Within the past 2 years, have middle managers/supervisors received training or consultation regarding **management** of a culturally/racially diverse workforce?
Yes   No

22. Within the past two years, have other staff received training or consultation regarding issues of working in a cultural/racial workforce diversity?

    Yes   No

23. Does the orientation for new employees routinely address issues of cultural/racial diversity in the workplace?

    Yes   No

24. Are proactive efforts made to assure integration of new employees from cultural/racial minority backgrounds into the organization (e.g., mentoring, buddy system, support groups, assignment to committees, etc.)?

    Yes   No

25. Are turnover rates for employees of color the same, higher, or lower than for comparable White employees?

    Employees of color have higher turnover rates than
       White employees.
    Employees of color have lower turnover rates than
       White employees.
    Employees of color have the same turnover rates as
       White employees.

26. Do performance evaluations and incentives for middle managers/supervisors tend to promote, limit, or fail to address performance based on cultural competency guidelines?

    Promote diversity
    Limit diversity
    Do not address diversity

27. Do performance evaluations and incentives for other employees tend to promote, limit, or fail to address performance based on cultural competency guidelines?

    Promote diversity
    Limit diversity
    Do not address diversity

28. With how many lawsuits involving employee allegations of discrimination based on race and/or ethnicity has your organization dealt in the past 2 years?

    None
    One
    Two
    Three
    Other: Write number here: _____

III. Services, Marketing, and Community Relations

29. Do senior managers and supervisors actively encourage development and marketing of services to culturally, linguistically, and racially diverse consumers/clients?
    Yes   No

30. In developing new **products** and services, does your organization **consciously** consider the cultural, racial, and linguistic characteristics of the potential customers/clients, including their specific needs, issues, and preferences?
    Yes   No

31. Does your company actively market its services to culturally and racially diverse consumers/clients, including targeted marketing efforts designed to appeal to the specific interests and preferences of different cultural/racial and linguistic groups?
    Yes   No

32. Do employees receive training or consultation in cross-cultural communication or relations?
    Yes   No

33. Is your organization's field ahead of, behind, or about on a par with the rest of society in its response to the increasing cultural/racial diversity of the United States?
    Ahead
    Behind
    About the same as the rest of society

IV. Public Relations

34. Do your organization's public relations efforts, including promotional materials, brochures, events, and the like, address and promote cultural/racial diversity?
    Yes   No

35. Do the organization's image and reputation in the larger community tend to encourage access to it by cultural/racial minority groups in the larger community?
    Yes   No

36. Are people with culturally/racially diverse characteristics featured in public relations materials?
    Yes   No

37. Are the people responsible for your company's Public Relations activities oriented to portraying the company as one that promotes cultural/racial diversity?
    Yes   No

38. Do the senior managers of the organization actively support PR activities that portray the company as one that promotes cultural/racial diversity?
    Yes   No

39. Are the organization's PR efforts normally reviewed and evaluated for their sensitivity and appeal to people of culturally and racially diverse backgrounds?
    Yes   No

V. Organizational Environment

40. Do your organization's internal communications systems (e.g., newsletters, memoranda, policy statements, reports, plans, and the like) address and promote cultural/racial diversity?
    Yes   No

41. Do the decor, photos, art, signs, and other aspects of your organization's offices and facilities tend to promote, limit, or not address cultural/racial diversity?
    Promote diversity
    Limit diversity
    Do not address diversity

42. Are the organization's special events (e.g., holiday celebrations, contests, forums, meetings, fundraisers, trips, etc.) planned in the context of their sensitivity to a culturally/racially diverse group of people?
    Yes   No

VI. Activities to Promote Effective Workforce Diversity

43. Has the owner/CEO and/or Board of Directors of your organization formally identified workforce diversity as an organization objective tied to business goals?
    Yes   No

44. During the past year has the owner/CEO and/or Board of Directors of your organization consistently supported and been involved personally in activities to promote workforce diversity?
    Yes   No

45. Has an employee in your organization been assigned specific formal responsibility to take the lead in promoting cultural/racial diversity in your organization?

    Yes   No

46. If your answer to question 39 was yes, how highly placed in the organization is the person assigned responsibility for promoting cultural/racial diversity?

    Senior manager
    Middle manager
    Other employee
    Not applicable/No person assigned

47. If your answer to question 39 was yes, is the assigned workforce diversity leader devoting half-time or more to this job role?

    Yes   No   Not applicable/No person assigned

48. Has the organization established an ongoing Workforce Diversity Workgroup that is responsible for working with the lead employee to assess the organization's needs and develop and carry out plans for improved workforce diversity?

    Yes   No

If your answer to question 42 was yes, is the membership of the Workforce Diversity Workgroup broadly representative of all employee groups in the organization?

    Yes   No   Not applicable/No workgroup

49. Has your organization carried out a formal assessment of the organization's status and needs in relation to workforce diversity?

    Yes   No

50. Has your organization developed a formal written plan to improve workforce diversity, including goals and objectives and an operational action plan with timelines?

    Yes   No

51. If your answer to question 45 was yes, to what extent has the formal written plan been implemented?

    Not implemented
    Currently being implemented
    Implementation complete
    Not applicable/no plan

VII. Organization/Personal Information

52. Name of organization: _____

53. Check your organization's industry below: (Check one.)
    (* Include list of industries here.)
    Industry 1
    Industry 2
    Other (Specify): _____

54. Is your group/organization* a separate corporate entity or a component of a larger organization? (Check one.)
    Separate corporation/business
    Component of larger corporation

    Based on your answer to this question, answer only *one* of the next two questions.

55. If your organization is a separate business/entity*, how many employees does your organization employ? (Check one.)
    Less than 10
    10 to 49
    50 to 99
    100 or more

56. If you are part of a component of a larger corporation*, how many employees are there in your component? And how many are there in the corporation as a whole? (Check one for each.)

Your component:	Total organization:
Less than 10	25 to 49
10 to 49	50 to 99
50 to 99	100 to 499
100 or more	500 or more

57. What is your own role in the organization*?
    CEO/owner
    Senior manager
    Middle manager
    Professional/technical
    Support/administrative
    Human resources (HR): management level or other
    Student/intern
    Other: (Specify)

58. What is your own cultural/racial background?
    African American
    Asian American/Pacific Islander

---

*Modify language relative to organization using the audit.

Hispanic/Latino
Native American
White/European American
Other: (Specify)
Additional comments: _____
_____
_____

Thank you for completing this survey.
Draft: For internal use only.

References

Abreu, J. M. (2001). Theory and research on stereotypes and perceptual bias: A didactic resource for multicultural counseling trainers. *The Counseling Psychologist, 29,* 87–512.

Acevedo, M. C., Reyes, C. J., Annett, R. D., & Lopez, E. M. (2003). Assessing language competence: Guidelines for assisting persons with limited proficiency in research and clinical settings. *Journal of Multicultural Counseling and Development, 31,* 192–222.

Achenbach, K., & Arthur, N. (2002). Experiential learning: Bridging theory to practice in multicultural counseling. *Guidance and Counseling, 17,* 39–46.

Allen, M. J. (n.d.). *Teaching nontraditional students.* Retrieved September 1, 2004, from Association for Psychological Science Web site: http://www.psychologicalscience.org/teaching/tips/tips_0900.html

Allport, G. W. (1954). *The nature of prejudice.* Cambridge, MA: Addison-Wesley.

American Psychological Association. (1990). *Guidelines for providers of psychological services to ethnic, linguistic, and culturally diverse populations.* Washington, DC: Author.

American Psychological Association. (2000). Guidelines for psychotherapy with lesbian, gay, and bisexual clients. *American Psychologist, 55,* 1440–1451.

American Psychological Association. (2001). *Criteria for practice guideline development and evaluation.* Washington, DC: Author.

American Psychological Association. (2002). Ethical principles of psychologists and code of conduct. *American Psychologist, 57,* 1060–1073.

American Psychological Association. (2003). Guidelines on multicultural education, training, research, practice, and organizational change for psychologists. *American Psychologist, 58,* 377–402.

American Psychological Association, Commission on Ethnic Minority Recruitment, Retention, and Training in Psychology. (1996a). *How to recruit and hire ethnic minority faculty.* Washington, DC: Author.

American Psychological Association, Commission on Ethnic Minority Recruitment, Retention, and Training in Psychology. (1996b). *Valuing diversity in faculty.* Washington, DC: Author.

American Psychological Association, Commission on Ethnic Minority Recruitment, Retention, and Training in Psychology. (1998). *Work group on student recruitment and retention.* Washington, DC: Author

American Psychological Association Research Office. (2002a). *Demographic characteristics of APA members by race/ethnicity; analyses of APA directory survey: 2000.* Washington, DC: American Psychological Association.

American Psychological Association Research Office. (2002b). *Race/ethnicity of APA members and APA governance members: Analyses of*

APA governance survey. Washington, DC: American Psychological Association.

American Psychological Association, Society of Consulting Psychology, Education, and Psychology. (1999). *Guidelines for education and training at the doctoral level in industrial–organizational psychology.* Washington, DC: Author.

Americans With Disabilities Act of 1990, 42 U.S.C.A. § 12101 *et seq.* (West 1993).

Antonio, A. L. (2002). Faculty of color reconsidered: Reassessing contributions to scholarship. *The Journal of Higher Education, 73,* 582–602.

Anzaldúa, G. (1987). *Borderlands/La frontera.* San Francisco: Aunt Lute Books.

Apter, M. J. (2003). Motivational styles and positioning theory. In R. Harré & F. Moghaddam (Eds.), *The self and others* (pp. 15–27). Westport, CT: Praeger.

Arizona Council of Human Service Providers. (2004, December). *Achieving a culturally competent and linguistically appropriate human service delivery system.* Phoenix, AZ: Author.

Armour, M. P., Bain, B., & Rubio, R. (2004). An evaluation study of diversity training for field instructors: A collaborative approach to enhancing cultural competence. *Journal of Social Work Education, 40,* 27–38.

Arredondo, P. (1996). *Successful diversity management initiatives.* Thousand Oaks, CA: Sage.

Arredondo, P. (2002). Counseling individuals from specialized, marginalized, and underserved groups. In P. Pedersen, J. G. Draguns, W. J. Lonner, & J. E. Trimble (Eds.), *Counseling across cultures* (5th ed., pp. 241–250). Thousand Oaks, CA: Sage.

Arredondo, P., & Arciniega, M. (2001). Strategies and techniques for counselor training based on the multicultural counseling competencies. *Journal of Multicultural Counseling and Development, 29,* 263–273.

Arredondo, P., & Glauner, T. (1992). *Personal dimensions of identity model.* Boston: Empowerment Workshops, Inc.

Arredondo, P., Shealy, C., Neale, M., & Winfrey, L. L. (2004). Consultation and interprofessional collaboration: Modeling for the future. *Journal of Clinical Psychology. Special Issue: Competencies Conference: Future Directions in Education and Credentialing in Professional Psychology, 60,* 787–800.

Arredondo, P., Toporek, R., Brown, S. P., Jones, J., Locke, D. C., Sanchez, J., et al. (1996). Operationalization of the multicultural counseling competencies. *Journal of Multicultural Counseling and Development, 24,* 42–78.

Arthur, N., & Achenbach, K. (2002). Developing multicultural counseling competencies through experiential learning. *Counselor Education and Supervision, 42,* 2–14.

Atkinson, D. R. (1985). A meta-review of research on multicultural counseling and psychotherapy. *Journal of Multicultural Counseling and Development, 13,* 138–153.

Atkinson, D. R., Morten, G., & Sue, D. W. (1989). A minority identity development model. In D. R. Atkinson, G. Morten, & D. W. Sue (Eds.), *Counseling American minorities* (pp. 35–52). Dubuque, IA: W. C. Brown.

Atkinson, D. R., Morten, G., & Sue, D. W. (1998). *Counseling American minorities* (5th ed.). Boston: McGraw-Hill.

Azevedo, A., Drost, E. A., & Mullen, M. R. (2002). Individualism and collectivism: Toward a strategy for testing measurement equivalence across culturally diverse groups. *Cross Cultural Management, 9,* 19–29.

Bache, R. M. (1919). Reaction time with reference to race. *Psychological Review, 2,* 475–486.

Benson, C. (2003). The unthinkable boundaries of self: The role of negative emotional boundaries in the formation, maintenance, and transformation of identities. In R. Harré & F. Moghaddam (Eds.), *The self and others* (pp. 61–84). Westport, CT: Praeger.

Bernal, M. E., & Castro, F. G. (1994). Are clinical psychologists prepared for service and research with ethnic minorities? Report of a decade of progress. *American Psychologist, 49,* 797–805.

Bernal, M. E., & Padilla, A. M. (1982). Status of minority curricula and training in clinical psychology. *American Psychologist, 37,* 780–787.

Bernal, M. E., Sirolli, A. A., Weisser, S. K., Ruis, J. A., Chamberlain, V. J., & Knight, G. P. (1999). Relevance of multicultural training to students' applications to clinical psychology programs. *Cultural Diversity and Ethnic Minority Psychology, 5,* 45–55.

Bidell, M. P., Turner, J. A., & Casas, J. M. (2002). First impressions count: Ethnic/racial and lesbian/gay/bisexual content of professional psychology application material. *Professional Psychology: Research and Practice, 33,* 97–103.

Boyd, V. S., Hunt, P. F., Kandell, J. J., & Lucas, M. S. (2003). Relationship between identity processing style and academic success in undergraduate students. *Journal of College Student Development, 44,* 155–167.

Boyd-Franklin, N. (2001). Using the multisystems model with an African American family: Cross-racial therapy and supervision. In S. H. McDaniel, D. P. Lusterman, & C. L. Philpot (Eds.), *Casebook for integrating family therapy: An ecosystemic approach* (pp. 395–400). Washington, DC: American Psychological Association.

Boyd-Franklin, N. (2003). *Black families in therapy: Understanding the African American experience* (2nd ed.). New York: Guilford Press.

Brewer, C. A., & Suchan, T. A. (2001). *Mapping Census 2000: The geography of U.S. diversity.* Washington, DC: U.S. Government Printing Office.

Brewer, M. B. (1991). The social self: On being the same and different at the same time. *Personality and Social Psychology Bulletin, 17,* 475–482.

Brewer, M. B. (1999). The psychology of prejudice: In-group love or out-group hate? *Journal of Social Issues, 55,* 429–444.

Brewer, M. B., & Brown, R. J. (1998). Intergroup relations. In D. T. Gilbert & S. T. Fiske (Eds.), *The handbook of social psychology* (Vol. 2, 4th ed., pp. 554–594). New York: McGraw-Hill.

Broverman, I., Vogel, S. R., Broverman, D. M., Clarkson, F. E., & Rosenkranz, P. W. (1972). Sex role stereotypes: A current appraisal. *Journal of Social Issues, 28,* 59–78.

Brown, M. T. (2004). The career development influence of family of origin: Considerations of race/ethnic group membership and class. *The Counseling Psychologist, 32,* 587–595.

Brown, S. P., Parham, T. A., & Yonker, R. (1996). Influence of a cross-cultural training course on racial identity attitudes of White women and men: Preliminary perspectives. *Journal of Counseling and Development, 74,* 510–516.

Butcher, J. N., Dahlstrom, W. G., Graham, J. R., Tellegen, A., & Kaemmer, B. (1989). *Minnesota Multiphasic Personality Inventory—2 (MMPI-2): Manual for administration and scoring.* Minneapolis: University of Minnesota Press.

Byars, A. M., & McCubbin, L. D. (2001). Trends in career development research with ethnoracial minorities: Prospects and challenges. In J. G. Ponterotto, J. M. Casas, L. A. Suzuki, & C. M. Alexander (Eds.), *Handbook of multicultural counseling* (2nd ed., pp. 633–654). Thousand Oaks, CA: Sage.

Carter, R. T. (1995). *The influence of race and racial identity in psychotherapy.* New York: Wiley.

Carter, R. T. (Ed.). (2005). *Handbook of racial–cultural psychology and counseling: Training and practice* (Vol. 2). Hoboken, NJ: Wiley.

Cassidy, S. (2004). Learning styles: An overview of theories, models, and measures. *Educational Psychology, 24,* 419–444.

Center for Teaching and Learning, University of North Carolina at Chapel Hill. (1997). *Teaching for inclusion: Diversity in the college classroom.* Retrieved September 1, 2004, from http://ctl.unc.edu/tfi2.html

Chesler, M., Wilson, M., & Malani, A. (1993). Perceptions of faculty behavior by students of color. *Michigan Journal of Political Science.*

Chien, W. W., & Banerjee, L. (2002). Caught between cultures: The young Asian American in therapy. In E. Davis-Russell (Ed.), *The California School of Professional Psychology handbook of multicultural education, research, intervention, and training* (pp. 210–220). San Francisco: Jossey-Bass.

Civil Rights Act of 1964, as amended, 42 U.S.C. § 2000E *et seq.* (1964).

Clark, K. B., & Clark, M. K. (1947). Racial identification and preference in Negro children. In T. M. Newcomb & E. L. Harley (Eds.), *Reading in social psychology* (pp. 169–178). New York: Holt, Reinhart & Winston.

Clarke, I., III. (2000). Extreme response style in multicultural research: An empirical investigation. *Journal of Social Behavior and Personality, 15,* 137–152.

Colby, A., & Foote, E. (1995). *Creating and maintaining a diverse faculty* (Report No. EDO-JC-95-06). Washington, DC: Office of Educational Research and Improvement. (ERIC Document Reproduction Service No. ED386261)

Combs, D. R., Penn, D. L., & Fenigstein, A. (2002). Ethnic differences in subclinical paranoia: An expansion of norms of the Paranoia Scale. *Cultural Diversity and Ethnic Minority Psychology, 8,* 248–256.

Constantine, M. (1998). Developing competence in multicultural assessment: Implications for counseling psychology training and practice. *The Counseling Psychologist, 6,* 922–929.

Constantine, M. (2001). Perspectives on multicultural supervision. *Journal of Multicultural Counseling and Development, 29,* 98–101.

Constantine, M. (2002). The intersection of race, ethnicity, gender, and social class in counseling: Examining selves in cultural contexts. *Journal of Multicultural Counseling and Development, 30,* 210–215.

Constantine, M., Ladany, N., Inman, A. G., & Ponterotto, J. G. (1996). Students' perceptions of multicultural training in counseling psychology programs. *Journal of Multicultural Counseling and Development, 24,* 241–253.

Costantino, G., Malgady, R. G., & Rogler, L. H. (1986). Cuento therapy: A culturally sensitive modality for Puerto Rican children. *Journal of Consulting and Clinical Psychology, 54,* 639–645.

Costantino, G., Malgady, R. G., & Rogler, L. H. (1994). Storytelling through pictures: Culturally sensitive psychotherapy for Hispanic children and adolescents. *Journal of Clinical Child Psychology, 23,* 13–20.

Council of National Psychological Associations for the Advancement of Ethnic Minority Interests. (2000). *Guidelines for research in ethnic minority communities.* Washington, DC: American Psychological Association.

Council of National Psychological Associations for the Advancement of Ethnic Minority Interests. (2003). *Psychological treatment of ethnic minority populations.* Washington, DC: American Psychological Association.

Cox, T. (1993). *Cultural diversity in organizations: Theory, practice, and research.* San Francisco: Berrett-Koehler.

Crocker, J., Major, B., & Steele, C. (1998). Social stigma. In D. T. Gilbert & S. T. Fiske (Eds.), *The handbook of social psychology* (4th ed., Vol. 2, pp. 504–553). New York: McGraw-Hill.

Cross, T., Barzon, B., Dennis, K., & Isaacs, M. (1989). *Toward a culturally competent system of care: A monograph on effective services for minority children who are severely emotionally disturbed* (Vol. 1). Washington, DC: Georgetown University Child Development Center.

Cross, W. E., Jr. (1991). *Shades of Black: Diversity in African American identity.* Philadelphia: Temple University Press.

Dadeghi, M., Fischer, J. M., & House, S. G. (2003). Ethical dilemmas in multicultural counseling. *Journal of Multicultural Counseling and Development, 31,* 179–191.

Dana, R. H. (1998). *Understanding cultural identity in intervention and assessment.* Thousand Oaks, CA: Sage.

D'Andrea, M., Daniels, J., & Heck, R. (1991). Evaluating the impact of multicultural counseling training. *Journal of Counseling and Development, 70,* 143–150.

Davis, O. I., Nakayama, T. K., & Martin, J. N. (2000). Current and future directions in ethnicity and methodology. *International Journal of Intercultural Relations, 24,* 525–539.

Derek Bok Center for Teaching and Learning, Harvard University. (2004). *Tips for teachers*

teaching in racially diverse college classrooms. Retrieved September 1, 2004, from http://www.bokcenter.harvard.edu/docs/TFTrace.html

Devlin, B., Fienberg, S. E., Resnick, D. P., & Roeder, K. (2002). Intelligence and success: Is it all in the genes? In J. M. Fish (Ed.), *Race and intelligence: Separating science from myth* (pp. 355–368). Mahwah, NJ: Erlbaum.

Diaz-Lázaro, C. M., & Cohen, B. B. (2001). Cross-cultural contact in counseling training. *Journal of Multicultural Counseling and Development, 29,* 41–56.

Dovidio, J. F., & Gaertner, S. L. (1998). On the nature of contemporary prejudice: The causes, consequences, and challenges of aversive racism. In J. L. Eberhardt & S. T. Fiske (Eds.), *Confronting racism: The problem and the response* (pp. 3–32). Thousand Oaks, CA: Sage.

Dovidio, J. F., Gaertner, S. L., & Validzic, A. (1998). Intergroup bias: Status, differentiation, and a common in-group identity. *Journal of Personality and Social Psychology, 75,* 109–120.

Dunn, R., Griggs, S. A., & Price, G. E. (1993). Learning styles of Mexican American and Anglo-American elementary school students. *Journal of Multicultural Counseling and Development, 21,* 237–247.

Egharevba, I. (2001). Researching an "Other" minority ethnic community: Reflections of a Black female researcher on the intersections of race, gender, and other power positions on the research process. *International Journal of Social Research Methodology: Theory and Practice, 4,* 225–241.

Ernhart, C. B., & Hebben, N. (1997). Intelligence and lead: The "known" is not known. *American Psychologist, 52,* 74.

Evans, C. (2004). Exploring the relationship between cognitive style and teaching style. *Educational Psychology, 24,* 509–530.

Evans, K. M., & Larrabee, M. J. (2002). Teaching the multicultural counseling competencies and revised career counseling competencies simultaneously. *Journal of Multicultural Counseling and Development, 30,* 21–39.

Falicov, C. J. (1999). Latino life cycle. In B. Carter & M. McGoldrick (Eds.), *The expanded life cycle: Individual, family, and social perspectives* (pp. 141–152). Boston: Allyn & Bacon.

Findlay, K. A., & Stephan, W. G. (2000). Improving intergroup relations: The effects of empathy on racial attitudes. *Journal of Applied Social Psychology, 30,* 1720–1737.

Fine, M., Weis, L., Powell, L. C., & Wong, L. M. (1997). *Off white: Readings on race, power, and society.* New York: Routledge.

Fischer, C. S., Hout, M., Jankowski, M. S., Lucas, S. R., Swidler, A., & Voss, K. (1996). *Inequality by design: Cracking the bell curve myth.* Princeton, NJ: Princeton University Press.

Fisher, C. B., Hoagwood, K., Boyce, C., Duster, T., Frank, D. A., Grisso, T., et al. (2002). Research ethics for mental health science involving ethnic minority children and youths. *American Psychologist, 57,* 1024–1040.

Fiske, S. T. (1993). Controlling other people. *American Psychologist, 48,* 621–628.

Fiske, S. T. (1998). Stereotyping, prejudice, and discrimination. In D. T. Gilbert & S. T. Fiske (Eds.), *The handbook of social psychology* (4th ed., Vol. 2, pp. 357–411). New York: McGraw-Hill.

Flores, M. T., & Carey, G. (Eds.). (2000). *Family therapy with Hispanics.* Needham Heights, MA: Allyn & Bacon.

Fontes, L. A. (1998). Ethics in family violence research: Cross-cultural issues. *Family Relations: Interdisciplinary Journal of Applied Family Studies, 47,* 53–61.

Fouad, N. A., & Brown, M. (2000). Race, ethnicity, culture, class, and human development. In S. D. Brown & R. W. Lent (Eds.), *Handbook of counseling psychology* (3rd ed., pp. 379–410). New York: Wiley.

Franklin, A. J. (2004). *From brotherhood to manhood: How Black men rescue their relationships and dreams from the invisibility syndrome.* New York: Wiley.

Frumkin, R. M. (1997). Significant neglected sociocultural and physical factors affecting intelligence. *American Psychologist, 52,* 76–77.

Fukuyama, M. A., & Ferguson, A. D. (2000). Lesbian, gay, and bisexual people of color: Understanding cultural complexity and managing multiple oppressions. In R. M. Perez, K. A. DeBord, & K. J. Bieschke (Eds.), *Handbook of counseling and psychotherapy with lesbian, gay, and bisexual clients* (pp. 81–106). Washington, DC: American Psychological Association.

Fukuyama, M. A., & Sevig, T. D. (1999). *Integrating spirituality into multicultural counseling.* Thousand Oaks, CA: Sage.

Gaertner, S. L., & Dovidio, J. F. (2000). *Reducing intergroup bias: The common ingroup identity model.* Philadelphia: Taylor & Francis.

Garrett, M. T., Garrett, J. T., & Brotherton, D. (2001). Inner circle/outer circle: A group technique based on Native American healing circles. *Journal for Specialists in Group Work, 26,* 17–30.

Garwick, A., & Auger, S. (2000). What do providers need to know about American Indian culture? Recommendations from urban Indian family caregivers. *Families, Systems, and Health, 18,* 177–190.

Gilligan, C. (1977). In a different voice: Women's conceptions of self and of morality. *Harvard Educational Review, 47,* 481–517.

Goodwin, R. (1996). A brief guide to cross-cultural psychological research. In J. Haworth (Ed.), *Psychological research: Innovative methods and strategies* (pp. 78–91). New York: Routledge.

Gorski, P. (2003). A guide for setting ground rules. In *Multicultural education and the Internet* (2nd ed.). Retrieved September 1, 2004, from http://www.mhhe.com/socscience/education/multi_new/activities/groundrules. html

Gould, S. J. (1994, November). The geometer of race. *Discover,* 65–69.

Grutter v. Bollinger, 539 U.S. (2003).

Guthrie, R. (1976). *Even the rats were white.* New York: Harper & Row.

Hall, G. C. N. (2001). Psychotherapy research with ethnic minorities: Empirical, ethical, and conceptual issues. *Journal of Consulting and Clinical Psychology, 69,* 502–510.

Hall, E. T. (1976). *Beyond culture.* Oxford, England: Anchor.

Hall, R. L., & Greene, B. (2003). Contemporary African American families. In L. B. Silverstein & T. J. Goodrich (Eds.), *Feminist family therapy: Empowerment in social context* (pp. 107–120). Washington, DC: American Psychological Association.

Halpern, D. F. (2004). *Creating cooperative learning environments.* Retrieved September 1, 2004, from Association for Psychological Science Web site: http://www.psychologicalscience.org/ teaching/tips/tips_0300.html

Hardiman, R. (1982). White identity development: A process oriented model for describing the racial consciousness of White Americans. *Dissertation Abstracts International, 43* (1), 104A. (UMI No. 8351619)

Harkness, S., & Keefer, C. H. (2000). Contributions of cross-cultural psychology to research and interventions in education and health. *Journal of Cross-Cultural Psychology, 31,* 92–109.

Harley, D. A., Jolivette, K., McCormick, K., & Tice, K. (2002). Race, class, and gender: A constellation of positionalities with implications for counseling. *Journal of Multicultural Counseling and Development, 30,* 216–238.

Harmon, L. W., Hansen, J. C., Borgen, F. H., & Hammer, A. L. (1994). *Strong Interest Inventory: Applications and technical guide.* Palo Alto, CA: Consulting Psychologists Press.

Harré, R., & Moghaddam, F. (Eds.). (2003). *The self and others.* Westport, CT: Praeger.

Harris, P. R., & Moran, R. T. (1987). *Managing cultural differences.* Houston, TX: Gulf Publishing.

Haslam, S. A. (2001). *Psychology in organizations: The social identity approach.* Thousand Oaks, CA: Sage.

Hedayat-Diba, Z. (2000). Psychotherapy with Muslims. In P. S. Richards & A. E. Bergin (Eds.), *Handbook of psychotherapy and religious diversity* (pp. 289–314). Washington, DC: American Psychological Association.

Helms, J. E. (1984). Toward a theoretical explanation of the effects of race on counseling: A Black and White model. *Counseling Psychologist, 12,* 153–165.

Helms, J. E. (1990). *Black and White racial identity: Theory, research, and practice.* New York: Greenwood Press.

Helms, J. E. (1995). An update of Helms's White and people of color racial identity models. In J. G. Ponterotto, J. M. Casas, L. A. Suzuki, & C. M. Alexander (Eds.), *Handbook of multicultural counseling* (pp. 181–198). Thousand Oaks, CA: Sage.

Helms, J. E. (2002). A remedy for the Black–White test-score disparity. *American Psychologist, 57,* 303–304.

Helms, J. E., & Cook, D. A. (1999). *Understanding race and culture in counseling and psychotherapy.* Needham Heights, MA: Allyn & Bacon.

Heppner, P. P., Kivlighan, D. M., Jr., & Wampold, B. E. (1999). *Research design in counseling* (2nd ed.). Belmont, CA: Brooks/Cole.

Herring, R. D. (1997). *Counseling diverse ethnic youth.* Fort Worth, TX: Harcourt Brace.

Herring, R. D. (1999). *Counseling with Native American Indians and Alaska Natives: Strategies for helping professionals.* Thousand Oaks, CA: Sage.

Herrnstein, R. J., & Murray, C. (1994). *The bell curve.* New York: Free Press.

Highlen, P. S. (1994). Ethnoracial diversity in doctoral programs of psychology: Challenges for the twenty-first century. *Applied and Preventive Psychology, 3,* 91–108.

Hofstede, G. (1980). *Culture's consequences.* London: Sage.

Hofstede, G., & McCrae, R. R. (2004). Personality and culture revisited: Linking traits and dimensions of culture. *Cross-Cultural Research: The Journal of Comparative Social Science, 38,* 52–88.

Hong, G. K., & Ham, M. D. C. (2001). *Psychotherapy and counseling with Asian American clients.* Thousand Oaks, CA: Sage.

hooks, b. (1994). *Teaching to transgress.* New York: Routledge.

Hurtado, S., Carter, D. F., & Kardia, D. (1998). The climate for diversity: Key issues for institutional self-study. *New Directions for Institutional Research, 25,* 53–63.

Ibarra, R. A. (2001). *Beyond affirmative action.* Madison: University of Wisconsin Press.

Ibrahim, F. A. (1984). Cross-cultural counseling and psychotherapy: An existential-psychological approach. *International Journal for the Advancement of Counselling, 7,* 159–169.

Ibrahim, F. A., & Cameron, S. C. (2005). Racial–cultural ethical issues in research. In R. T. Carter (Ed.), *Racial–cultural psychology and counseling: Theory and research* (Vol. 1, pp. 391–413). New York: Wiley.

Jackson, L. C. (1999). Ethnocultural resistance to multicultural training: Students and faculty. *Cultural Diversity and Ethnic Minority Psychology, 5,* 27–36.

Johnston, W. B., & Packer, A. E. (1987). *Workforce 2000.* Indianapolis, IN: Hudson Institute.

Jones, H. (2004). A research-based approach on teaching to diversity. *Journal of Instructional Psychology, 31,* 12–19.

Judy, R. W., & D'Amico, C. (1997). *Workforce 2020.* Indianapolis, IN: Hudson Institute.

Katz, J. H. (1985). The sociopolitical nature of counseling. *The Counseling Psychologist, 13,* 615–624.

Keiley, M. K., Dolbin, M., Hill, J., Karuppaswamy, N., Liu, T., Natrajan, R., et al. (2002). The cultural genogram: Experiences from within marriage and family therapy training programs. *Journal of Marital and Family Therapy, 28,* 165–178.

Keller, E. F. (1982). Feminism and science. *Signs, 7,* 589–602.

Kelley, T. L. (1915). A study of high school and university grades with reference to their intercorrelations and the causes of elimination. *Journal of Educational Psychology, 6,* 365–367.

Kim, B. S. K., Atkinson, D. R., & Umemoto, D. (2001). Asian cultural values and the counseling process: Current knowledge and directions for future research. *The Counseling Psychologist, 29,* 570–603.

Kim, B. S. K., & Lyons, H. Z. (2003). Experiential activities and multicultural counseling competence training. *Journal of Counseling and Development, 81,* 400–408.

Kirkpatrick, L. (2001). *Multicultural strategies for community colleges: Expanding faculty diversity* (Report No. EDO-JC-01–05). Washington, DC: Office of Educational Research and Improvement. (ERIC Document Reproduction Service No. ED455902)

Kite, M. E., Russo, N. F., Brehm, S. S., Fouad, N. A., Hall, C. C., Hyde, J. S., et al. (2001). Women psychologists in academe: Mixed progress, unwarranted complacency. *American Psychologist, 56,* 1080–1098.

Kluckhohn, C., & Kroeber, A. L. (1963). *Culture: A critical review of concepts and definitions.* New York: Vintage Books.

Kluckhohn, F. R., & Strodbeck, F. L. (1961). *Variations in value orientations.* Evanston, IL: Row, Peterson.

Korchin, S. J. (1980). Clinical psychology and minority problems. *American Psychologist, 35,* 262–269.

Korman, M. (1974). National conference on levels and patterns of professional training in psychology: The major themes. *American Psychologist, 29,* 441–449.

LaFromboise, T. D., & Dizon, M. R. (2003). American Indian children and adolescents. In J. T. Gibbs & L. N. Huang (Eds.), *Children of color: Psychological interventions with culturally diverse youth* (pp. 45–90). San Francisco: Jossey-Bass.

LaFromboise, T. D., & Foster, S. L. (1992). Multicultural training: Scientist-practitioner model and methods. *The Counseling Psychologist, 20,* 472–489.

LaFromboise, T. D., & Jackson, M. (1996). MCT theory and Native American populations. In D. W. Sue, A. E. Ivey, & P. B. Pedersen (Eds.), *A theory of multicultural counseling and therapy* (pp. 192–203). Pacific Grove, CA: Brooks/Cole.

LaFromboise, T. D., Trimble, J. E., & Mohatt, G. V. (1998). Counseling intervention and American Indian tradition: An integrative approach. In D. R. Atkinson, G. Morten, & D. W. Sue (Eds.), *Counseling American minorities* (5th ed., pp. 159–182). New York: McGraw-Hill.

Langman, P. F. (1998). *Jewish issues in multiculturalism: A handbook for educators and clinicians.* Northvale, NJ: Jason Aronson.

Larkin, T. J., & Larkin, S. (1994). *Communicating change.* New York: McGraw Hill.

Lee, R. M., Chalk, L., Conner, S. E., Kawasaki, N., Jannetti, A., LaRue, T., et al. (1999). The status of multicultural counseling training at counseling internship sites. *Journal of Multicultural Counseling and Development, 27,* 58–74.

Lehman, D. R., Chiu, C., & Schaller, M. (2004). Psychology and culture. *Annual Review of Psychology, 55,* 689–714.

Lowe, S. M., & Mascher, J. (2001). The role of sexual orientation in multicultural counseling: Integrating bodies of knowledge. In J. G. Ponterotto, J. M. Casas, L. A. Suzuki, & C. M. Alexander (Eds.), *Handbook of multicultural counseling* (2nd ed., pp. 755–778). Thousand Oaks, CA: Sage.

Lynn, R. (1997). Direct evidence for a genetic basis for black-white differences in IQ. *American Psychologist, 52,* 73–74.

Manese, J. E., Wu., J. T., & Nepomuceno, C. A. (2001). The effect of training on multicultural counseling competencies: An exploratory study over a 10-year period. *Journal of Multicultural Counseling and Development, 29,* 31–40.

Marin, G., & Marin, B. V. (1991). *Research with Hispanic populations.* Thousand Oaks, CA: Sage.

Markus, H. R., & Kitayama, S. (2001). The cultural construction of self and emotion: Implications for social behavior. In W. G. Perrod (Ed.), *Emotions in social psychology: Essential reading* (pp. 119–137). Philadelphia: Brunner-Routledge.

McCreary, M. L., & Walker, V. D. (2001). Teaching multicultural counseling prepracticum. *Teaching of Psychology, 28,* 195–198.

McDowell, T., Fang, S., Brownlee, K., Young, C. G., & Khanna, A. (2002). Transforming an MFT program: A model for enhancing diversity. *Journal of Marital and Family Therapy, 28,* 179–191.

McGlynn, A. P. (1999). Innovations and programs. Teaching strategies that promote equal opportunity: I. Collaborative learning communities. *The Hispanic Outlook in Higher Education, 10,* 19–22.

McGoldrick, M., Giordano, J., & Pearce, J. K. (Eds.). (1996). *Ethnicity and family therapy* (2nd ed.). New York: Guilford.

McIntosh, P. (1989, July/August). White privilege: Unpacking the invisible knapsack. *Peace and Freedom,* 8–10.

Melnick, M. (1997). Methodological errors in the prediction of ability. *American Psychologist, 52,* 74–75.

Messick, S. (1995). Validity of psychological assessment: Validation of inferences from persons' responses and performances as scientific inquiry into score meaning. *American Psychologist, 50*, 741–749.

Middleton, R. A., Rollins, C. W., & Harley, D. A. (1999). The historical and political context of the civil rights of persons with disabilities: A multicultural perspective for counselors. *Journal of Multicultural Counseling and Development, 27*, 105–120.

Mio, J. S., & Iwamasa, G. Y. (2003). *Culturally diverse mental health: The challenges of research and resistance.* New York: Brunner-Routledge.

Morgan, G. (1997). *Images of organizations* (2nd ed.). Thousand Oaks, CA: Sage.

Naglieri, J. A. (1997). IQ: Knowns and unknowns, hits and misses. *American Psychologist, 52*, 75–76.

National Center on Education Statistics. (2003). *Postsecondary education statistics.* Retrieved January 21, 2005, from http://nces.ed.gov/quicktables/Detail.asp?Key=1120

Neisser, U., Boodoo, G., Bouchard, T. J., Jr., Boykin, A. W., Brody, N., Ceci, S. J., et al. (1996). Intelligence: Knowns and unknowns. *American Psychologist, 51*, 77–101.

Niemann, Y. F. (2001). Stereotypes about Chicanas and Chicanos: Implications for counseling. *The Counseling Psychologist, 29*, 55–90.

Padilla, A. M. (1995). (Ed.). *Hispanic psychology: Critical issues in theory and research.* Thousand Oaks, CA: Sage.

Parham, T. A., & Helms, J. E. (1985). Attitudes of racial identity and self-esteem of Black students: An exploratory investigation. *Journal of College Student Personnel, 26*, 143–147.

Park, C. C. (2001). Learning style preferences of Armenian, African, Hispanic, Hmong, Korean, Mexican, and Anglo students in American secondary schools. *Learning Environments Research, 4*, 175–191.

Parrott, W. G. (2003). Positioning and the emotions. In R. Harré & F. Moghaddam (Eds.), *The self and others* (pp. 29–43). Westport, CT: Praeger.

Pinderhughes, E. (1992). *Understanding race, ethnicity, and power: The key to efficacy in clinical practice.* New York: Free Press.

Poe, R. E. (2004). *Hitting a nerve: When touchy subjects come up in class.* Retrieved September 1, 2004, from Association for Psychological Science Web site: http://www.psychologicalscience.org/teaching/tips/tips_1100.html

Ponterotto, J. G. (1997). Multicultural counseling training: A competency model and national survey. In D. B. Pope-Davis & H. L. K. Coleman (Eds.), *Multicultural counseling competencies: Assessment, education and training, and supervision* (pp. 111–130). Thousand Oaks, CA: Sage.

Pope-Davis, D. B., & Ottavi, T. M. (1994). Examining the association between self-reported multicultural counseling competencies and demographic variables among counselors. *Journal of Counseling and Development, 72*, 651–654.

Prendes-Lintel, M. (2001). A working model in counseling recent refugees. In J. G. Ponterotto, J. M. Casas, L. A. Suzuki, & C. M. Alexander (Eds.), *Handbook of multicultural counseling* (2nd ed., pp. 729–752). Thousand Oaks, CA: Sage.

Priester, P. E., Jackson-Bailey, C. M., Jones, J. E., Jordan, E. X., & Metz, A. J. (2004). *An analysis of content and instructional strategies in APA accredited counseling psychology multicultural counseling courses.* Unpublished manuscript, University of Wisconsin–Milwaukee.

Quintana, S. M., & Bernal, M. E. (1995). Ethnic minority training in counseling psychology: Comparisons with clinical psychology and proposed standards. *The Counseling Psychologist, 23*, 102–121.

Quintana, S. M., Troyano, N., & Taylor, G. (2001). Cultural validity and inherent challenges in quantitative methods for multicultural research. In J. G. Ponterotto, J. M. Casas, L. A. Suzuki, & C. M. Alexander (Eds.), *Handbook of multicultural counseling* (2nd ed., pp. 604–630). Thousand Oaks, CA: Sage.

Ramirez, M., & Castañeda, A. (1974). *Cultural democracy, bicognitive development, and education.* New York: Academic Press.

Reardon, P., & Prescott, S. (1977). Sex as reported in a recent sample of psychological research. *Psychology of Women Quarterly, 2*, 157–161.

Reed, T. E. (1997). "The genetic hypothesis": It was not tested but it could have been. *American Psychologist, 52*, 77–78.

Reid, L. D., & Radhakrishnan, P. (2003). Race matters: The relation between race and general campus climate. *Cultural Diversity and Ethic Minority Psychology, 9*, 263–275.

Renzulli, J. S., & Dai, D. Y. (2001). Abilities, interests, and styles as aptitudes for learning: A person–situation interaction perspective. In R. J. Sternberg & L. Zhang (Eds.), *Per-*

spectives on thinking, learning, and cognitive styles (pp. 23–46). Mahwah, NJ: Erlbaum.

Ridley, C. (1995). *Overcoming unintentional racism in counseling and therapy: A practitioner's guide to intentional intervention.* Thousand Oaks, CA: Sage.

Ridley, C., Hill, C., & Li, L. (1998). Revisiting and refining the multicultural assessment procedure. *The Counseling Psychologist, 6,* 939–947.

Ridley, C., & Thompson, C. E. (1999). Managing resistance to diversity training: A social systems perspective. In M. S. Kiselica (Ed.), *Confronting prejudice and racism during multicultural training.* Alexandria, VA: American Counseling Association.

Rogers, M. R., Hoffman, M. A., & Wade, J. (1998). Notable multicultural training in APA-approved counseling psychology and school psychology programs. *Cultural Diversity and Mental Health, 4,* 212–226.

Rogler, L. H. (1999). Methodological sources of cultural insensitivity in mental health research. *American Psychologist, 64,* 424–433.

Root, M. P. P. (1999). The biracial baby boom: Understanding ecological constructions of racial identity in the 21st century. In R. H. Sheets & E. R. Hollins (Eds.), *Racial and ethnic identity in school practices: Aspects of human development* (pp. 67–89). Mahwah, NJ: Erlbaum.

Ruiz, A. S. (1990). Ethnic identity: Crisis and resolution. *Journal of Multicultural Counseling and Development, 18,* 29–40.

Saldana, D. (1995). Acculturative stress: Minority status and distress. In A. M. Padilla (Ed.), *Hispanic psychology* (pp. 43–56). Thousand Oaks, CA: Sage.

Samuda, R. J. (1998). *Psychological testing of American minorities.* Thousand Oaks, CA: Sage.

Sandoval, J., Frisby, C. L., Geisinger, K. F., Scheuneman, J. D., & Grenier, J. R. (Eds.). (1998). *Test interpretation and diversity: Achieving equity in assessment.* Washington, DC: American Psychological Association.

Santiago-Rivera, A., Arredondo, P., & Gallardo-Cooper, M. (2002). *Counseling Latinos and la familia: A practitioner's guide.* Thousand Oaks, CA: Sage.

Saunders, S., & Kardia D. (n.d). *Creating inclusive college classroom.* Retrieved September 1, 2004, from University of Michigan, Center for Research on Learning and Teaching Web site: http://www.crlt.umich.edu/gsis/P3_1.html

Schwabacher, S. (1972). Male versus female representation in psychological research: An examination of the *Journal of Personality and Social Psychology,* 1970, 1971. *Catalog of Selected Documents in Psychology, 2,* 20–21.

Seligman, M. E. P. (1975). *Helplessness: On depression, development, and death.* San Francisco: Freeman.

Senge, P. (1990). Catalyzing systems thinking within organizations. In F. Massarik (Ed.), *Advances in organization development* (Vol. 1, pp. 197–246). Westport, CT: Ablex Publishing.

Sevig, T., & Etzkorn, J. (2001). Transformative training: A year-long multicultural counseling seminar for graduate students. *Journal of Multicultural Counseling and Development, 29,* 57–72.

Simpson, J. B. (1988). *Simpson's contemporary quotations.* Boston: Houghton Mifflin.

Smart, J. F., & Smart, D. W. (1995). Acculturative stress of Hispanics: Loss and challenge. *Journal of Counseling and Development, 73,* 390–396.

Smith, D. G., Turner, C. S., Osei-Kofi, N., & Richards, S. (2004). Interrupting the usual: Successful strategies for hiring diverse faculty. *The Journal of Higher Education, 75,* 133–160.

Smith, E. M. (1985). Ethnic minorities: Life stress, social support, and mental health issues. *Counseling Psychologist, 13,* 537–579.

Speight, S. L., Thomas, A. J., Kennel, R. G., & Anderson, M. E. (1995). Operationalizing multicultural training in doctoral programs and internships. *Professional Psychology: Research and Practice, 26,* 401–406.

Spencer, M. B., Kim, S., & Marshall, S. (1987). Double stratification and psychological risk: Adaptational processes and school achievement of Black children. *Journal of Negro Education, 56,* 77–87.

Spengler, P. M. (1998). Multicultural assessment and a scientist–practitioner model of psychological assessment. *The Counseling Psychologist, 6,* 930–938.

SSPS, Inc. (2005). Statistical Package for the Social Sciences (Version 13.1, for Windows) [Computer software]. Chicago: SPSS.

Steele, C. M. (1997). A threat in the air: How stereotypes shape intellectual identity and performance. *American Psychologist, 52,* 613–629.

Strauss, A., & Corbin, J. (1998). *Basics of qualitative research* (2nd ed.). Thousand Oaks, CA: Sage.

Sue, D. W. (1977). Counseling the culturally different: A conceptual analysis. *Personnel and Guidance Journal, 55,* 422–425.

Sue, D. W. (1983). Confronting ourselves: The white and racial/ethnic minority researcher. *The Counseling Psychologist, 21,* 244–249.

Sue, D. W. (2001). Multidimensional facets of cultural competence. *The Counseling Psychologist, 29,* 790–821.

Sue, D. W., Arredondo, P., & McDavis, R. J. (1992). Multicultural counseling competencies and standards: A call to the profession. *Journal of Counseling and Development, 70,* 477–483.

Sue, D. W., Bernier, J., Durran, M., Feinberg, L., Pedersen, P., Smith, E., et al. (1982). Position paper: Multicultural counseling competencies. *The Counseling Psychologist, 10,* 45–52.

Sue, D. W., Carter, R. T., Casas, J. M., Fouad, N. A., Ivey, A. E., Jensen, M., et al. (1998). *Multicultural counseling competencies: Individual and organizational development.* Thousand Oaks, CA: Sage.

Sue, D. W., & Sue, S. (1977). Ethnic minorities: Failures and responsibilities of the social sciences. *Journal of Non-White Concerns in Personnel and Guidance, 5,* 99–106.

Sue, D. W., & Sue, D. (1999). *Counseling the culturally different: Theory and practice* (3rd ed.). New York: Wiley.

Sue, D. W., & Sue, D. (2003). *Counseling the culturally diverse* (4th ed.). Hoboken, NJ: Wiley.

Sue, S. (1999). Science, ethnicity, and bias: Where have we gone wrong? *American Psychologist, 54,* 1070–1077.

Suzuki, L. A., Prendes-Lintel, M., Wertlieb, L., & Stallings, A. (1999). Exploring multicultural issues using qualitative methods. In M. Kopala & L. A. Suzuki (Eds.), *Using qualitative methods in psychology* (pp. 123–133). Thousand Oaks, CA: Sage.

Swim, J., & Stangor, C. (1998). *Prejudice: The target's perspective.* San Diego, CA: Academic Press.

Thiederman, S. (1991). *Profiting in America's multicultural marketplace: How to do business across cultural lines.* New York: Lexington Books.

Thomas, M. B. (1986). The use of expectancy theory and the theory of learned helplessness in building upon strengths of ethnic minorities: The Black experience in the United States. *International Journal for the Advancement of Counselling, 9,* 371–379.

Thomas, R. R. (1991). *Beyond race and gender: Unleashing the power of your total workforce by managing diversity.* New York: AMACOM.

Thomas, R. R. (1996). *Redefining diversity.* New York: American Management Association.

Tien, L., & Olson, K. (2003). Confucian past, conflicted present: Working with Asian American families. In L. B. Silverstein & T. J. Goodrich (Eds.), *Feminist family therapy: Empowerment in social context* (pp. 135–145). Washington, DC: American Psychological Association.

Title IX, Education Amendments of 1972 (Title 20 U.S.C. §§ 1681–1688).

Triandis, H. C. (2001). Individualism–collectivism and personality. *Journal of Personality, 69,* 907–924.

Triandis, H. C., & Suh, E. M. (2002). Cultural influences on personality. *Annual Review of Psychology, 53,* 133–160.

Uomoto, J. M. (1986). Examination of psychological distress in ethnic minorities from a learned helplessness framework. *Professional Psychology: Research and Practice, 17,* 448–453.

U.S. Census Bureau. (2004). *U.S. Census 2004.* Available from U.S. Census Bureau Web site: http://www.census.gov

U.S. Department of Health and Human Services. (1999). *Mental health: A report of the Surgeon General.* Rockville, MD: Author.

U.S. Department of Health and Human Services. (2000). *Mental health: Culture, race and ethnicity—A supplement to mental health: A report of the Surgeon General.* Rockville, MD: Author.

U.S. Department of Health and Human Services. (2001). *Mental health: Culture, race, ethnicity—A supplement to mental health: A report of the Surgeon General.* Rockville, MD: Author.

Utsey, S. O., & Gernat, C. A. (2002). White racial identity attitudes and the go defense mechanisms used by White counselor trainees in racially provocative counseling situations. *Journal of Counseling and Development, 80,* 475–483.

Utsey, S. O., McCarthy, E., Eukanks, R., & Adrian, G. (2002). White racism and suboptimal psychological functioning among White Americans: Implications for counseling and prejudice prevention. *Journal of Multicultural Counseling and Development, 30,* 81–95.

Vandiver, B. J. (2001). Psychological nigrescence revisited: Introduction and overview. *Journal of Multicultural Counseling and Development, 29,* 165–173.

Velden, M. (1997). The heritability of intelligence: Neither known nor unknown. *American Psychologist, 52,* 72–73.

Warner, J. C. (2003). Group therapy with Native Americans: Understanding essential differences. *Group, 27,* 191–202.

Westermeyer, J., & Janca, A. (1997). Language, culture, and psychopathology: Conceptual and methodological issues. *Transcultural Psychiatry, 34,* 291–311.

Wierzbicka, A. (1994). Emotional, language, and cultural scripts. In S. Kitayama & H. R. Markus (Eds.), *Emotion and culture* (pp. 133–196). Washington, DC: American Psychological Association.

Wolsko, C., Park, B., Judd, C. M., & Wittenbrink, B. (2000). Framing interethnic ideology: Effects of multicultural and color-blind perspectives on judgments of groups and individuals. *Journal of Personality and Social Psychology, 78,* 635–654.

Wrenn, G. C. (1962). The culturally-encapsulated counselor. *Harvard Educational Review, 32,* 444–449.

Index

About the Authors

Nadya A. Fouad, PhD, is a professor in the Department of Educational Psychology and training director in counseling psychology at the University of Wisconsin—Milwaukee (UWM). In 2003, she was recipient of the John Holland Award for Outstanding Achievement in Career and Personality Research. Dr. Fouad was president of Division 17 (Society of Counseling Psychology) of the American Psychological Association (APA) in 2000–2001, is cointerim vice president for Communications, and previously served as vice president for Diversity and Public Interest of Division 17 (1996–1999). She is editor-elect of *The Counseling Psychologist* and is chair of the Council of Counseling Psychology Training Programs (2003–2007). She serves on the editorial boards of the *Journal of Counseling Psychology,* the *Journal of Vocational Behavior, Career Development Quarterly,* and the *Journal of Career Assessment.* Dr. Fouad chaired the UWM Task Force on Climate for Women and the APA Task Force for Women in Academe. Dr. Fouad has published articles and chapters on cross-cultural vocational assessment, career development of women and racial–ethnic minorities, interest measurement, cross-cultural counseling, and race and ethnicity. She has served as cochair (with Patricia Arredondo) of the writing team for the "Guidelines on Multicultural Education, Training, Research, Practice, and Organizational Change for Psychologists," which were approved by the APA in August 2002 and were published in the *American Psychologist* in May 2003.

Patricia Arredondo, EdD, is senior associate vice president for University Undergraduate Initiatives and professor of counseling/counseling psychology at Arizona State University. She is known for her scholarship in the areas of multicultural competencies, organizational diversity management, and Latino psychology. Dr. Arredondo has served as president of national associations including Division 45 (Society for the Psychological Study of Ethnic Minority Issues) of the American Psychological Association, the American Counseling Association, the National Latina/o Psychological Association, and the Association of Multicultural Counseling and Development. She is a fellow of Divisions 17 and 45 of the American Psychological Association and was recognized as a "Living Legend" for her contributions to multicultural counseling by the American Counseling Association. Dr. Arredondo holds an honorary degree from the University of San Diego.